AF497723

ÆSCHYLUS

IN ENGLISH VERSE.

PART III.

AGAMEMNON.
CHOËPHOROE, or THE MOURNERS.
EUMENIDES, or THE RECONCILIATION.

BY

ARTHUR S. WAY, D.Lit.

AUTHOR OF
TRANSLATIONS INTO ENGLISH VERSE OF HOMER'S ILIAD AND ODYSSEY,
THE TRAGEDIES OF EURIPIDES, ETC.

London:
MACMILLAN AND CO., LIMITED
ST. MARTIN'S STREET, LONDON
1908

BARNICOTT AND PEARCE,
PRINTERS.

AGAMEMNON.

ARGUMENT.

FOR *three generations the House of Atreus lay under a curse, the Curse of Kindred Blood. For when Atreus was king of Mycenæ, Thyestes, his brother, corrupted the king's wife, and with her plotted Atreus' ruin. So Atreus sought to slay him, and he fled from the land. But when after many days Thyestes returned, Atreus feigned to be reconciled to him, and bade him to a feast. But therein he had the flesh of Thyestes' own children set before their father, who unwittingly ate thereof. He, when he knew the truth, called down upon Atreus' house this curse, that kindred should still slay kindred to the third generation. And it came to pass that when Agamemnon, the son of Atreus, was made captain of the host of Greece which was to sail against Troy, he provoked the wrath of Artemis, and the goddess held the fleet wind-bound at Aulis, till he made atonement by sacrificing his own daughter, Iphigeneia. For this cause his wife Klytemnestra hated him, and conspired with Ægisthus, Thyestes' son, with whom she lived in adultery, to destroy him when he should come home from the war. So they prepared beacons upon the mountains between Troy and Greece, and set a watchman to watch for the first token that these should give of the fall of Troy.*

And herein is told how Agamemnon came home from the war, and by what means his wife compassed his murder.

DRAMATIS PERSONÆ.

AGAMEMNON, *King of Mycenæ.*

KLYTEMNESTRA, *wife to Agamemnon.*

KASSANDRA, *a prophetess, Daughter of Priam, King of Troy, and captive of Agamemnon.*

ÆGISTHUS, *son of Thyestes, co-plotter with Klytemnestra.*

WATCHMAN.

HERALD.

CHORUS, *consisting of Elders of Mycenæ.*

SCENE :—In front of the palace of Agamemnon.

AGAMEMNON.

WATCHMAN.

I PRAY the Gods for riddance from these toils,
The long lapse of this watch of years, wherein
Couched doglike, elbow-propped, on the Atreids' roof,
I have learnt by heart the muster of night's stars,
Yea, those which bring men winter and summer-tide,
Bright potentates throned in the firmament
As stars—their settings and their risings know.
Now watch I for the token of the torch,
The splendour of fire that brings us word from Troy,
Brings tidings of her fall: for so constrains   10
Yon woman's heart man-mettled, aye expectant.
When on this couch night-wildered, dew-bedrenched,
I lie, a couch not visited of dreams,—
For Fear in Sleep's stead is my chamberlain,
That unafraid I cannot close mine eyes,—
Then, when I think to sing or hum a stave,
As who should shred him sleep-dispelling herbs,
Then weep I, and bemoan this house's plight,
Its foul misrule, far other than of old.

Now come with blessing, O release from toil,   20
Fire of glad tidings flashing through the gloom !
(A beacon-light gleams out on the northern sky-line.)
Hail, torch of night, who tossest high a gleam
As dayspring fair, that meaneth many a dance
Arrayed in Argos, for this triumph's sake !
What ho ! what ho !
Lo, I will certify Agamemnon's wife.
So from her couch leaping in haste shall she
Shrill forth a shout in welcome to yon torch—
If Ilium-town have fallen in very deed
As yonder herald-beacon manifests.   30
Myself will dance the prelude thereunto ;
For I will count my lord's good-hap mine own—
The thrice-six[1] cast me by the beacon-blaze.
Ah, be it mine to upbear with this my hand
My lord's dear hand when he returneth home !
No more—upon my tongue treads heavily
The ox.[2] The house's self, could it find voice
Would cry too plainly. I to such as know
Speak, nothing loth : for others—I forget.

[*Exit.*

Enter Chorus.

CHORUS.

This is the tenth of the years since to plead at the
      War-god's bar   40
Rose in his might against Priam the king Menelaus :
      to war

---

  1. The luckiest possible throw when playing, as was usual,
with three dice.

  2. A rustic metaphor, equivalent to 'my lips are sealed.'

Went Agamemnon beside him: of Zeus were their
    thrones, even twain ;
Twain were their sceptres of royalty: like unto steeds
    that strain
Under one yoke were Atreides' sons: from our land
    led they
Galleys a thousand that wafted to aid them a warrior-
    array,
Shouting the fury of fight from their souls: it was
    fierce as the sound
Ringing through desolate places when vultures are
    wheeling round
High o'er their eyry in anguish for nestlings afar from
    it torn,   50
Heavily beating like oars the broad pinions whereon
    they are borne,
Hungry for tendance of nurslings whereof they are left
    forlorn—
Yet not alone; for Apollo or Zeus or the Wildwood-king,
Hearing the wail of the aliens that lodge in their city
    upring,
Haply a lingering vengeance, yet sure, on the spoilers
    shall bring.
So hath a mightier Zeus, the Warder of Strangers,
    sped   60
Atreus' sons, for her sake whom full many a man
    would have wed,
Hard on the track of the prince Alexander, ordaining
    for these
Many a desperate grapple where fainted men's
    strength, and their knees
Bowed, and were dashed in the dust, and the shafts
    of the war-spears crashed

Splintered in twain, where the battle-fronts Trojan
　　and Danaan clashed.
Now is the end—*as it is* ; and the doom foreordained
　　is fulfilled.
Never by secret burnt-sacrifice, not by drink-offerings
　　spilled,
Neither by tears, shall the Wrath for the rites dese-
　　crated be stilled.　　　　　　　　　　　　70

We, whom the eld-withered frame made of little
　　account, when went
Over the sea battle-helpers, abide ; for our strength
　　forspent,
Frail as the strength of a babe, o'er the staff bowed,
　　wearily creeps ;—
Yea, for the blood of the child, in the tender bosom
　　that leaps,
Strengthless as eld is at first : the War-god therein
　　hath no place :
So, when its leafage is sere, totters eld on its three-
　　footed ways,　　　　　　　　　　　　80
Nowise more strong than a child, as a dream—as a
　　daydream, it strays.

But thou, O Klytemnestra, Argos' Queen,
　　Tyndareus' child, what is to do ?
What hath befallen ?　What hast heard or seen ?
　　What tidings have won through,

That thy commandment all the city round
　　Bids sacrifice ?　The Gods that sway
Yon burg—the Gods on high, beneath the ground—
　　Heaven-dwelling Ones, and they

That rule the mart—lo, all their altars blaze   90
   With gifts thereon : to left, to right
The flaming offerings high as heaven upraise
   Thanksgiving-hands of light,

Whereto the soft, the uncontaminate
   Suasion of oil is ministering,
Of that pure chrism from the inviolate
   Hid treasury of the King.

Tell us hereof whate'er thou canst declare,
   Whose utterance crosses not Heaven's will ;
So bring assuaging of this fever of care
   That darkly now bodes ill,   100

And now, at sight of yonder sacrifice,
   Hope's radiant smile thrusts back again
Relentless fear, whose nightmare burden lies
   On hearts deep-gnawed by pain.

(Str. 1)

It is mine to chant the victory fated,
   And the omen that came in the wayfaring
Of the mighty heroes ; for unabated
By years is the God's inspiration, and mated
   Therewith is the trust in whose strength I sing.
I sing how the vehement eagle-omen
   Sped onward with spear and avenging hand
Achaia's twin-throned lords on the foemen,
Sped the one-souled chiefs of the stalwart yeomen 110
   Of Hellas against the Teukrian land ;
How the kings of the birds to the kings of the
     galleys—
   One erne black, one with the tail white-gleaming—
Appeared on the spear-hand hard by the palace

On a spot set clear for all men's discerning,
  Rending a hare with her brood yet teeming,
Which was stopped in her last swift frenzied turning.
    Woe's me and alas for doom's hid net!   [120
    Yet oh, may the Right be triumphant yet!

(Ant. 1)

Then looked on the warrior Atreids, heeding
  Their diverse natures with clear calm eye,
The seer of the host, and the ravin-feeding
Eagles he knew for the captains leading
  The host; and in vision thus did he cry:
' By them that on this war-path have wended
  Shall the city of Priam be taken at last,
And all the wealth that her towers defended
For enriching of them that her cause befriended
  Shall Doom with ravaging hands lay waste.   130
Yet the battle-curb of the guilty city—
  Be it not overclouded, untimely stricken
By wrath divine; for with jealous pity
For that wretched hare, looked Artemis lowering
  On her Sire's winged hounds, that, ere life might
    quicken
To the birth, were mother and brood devouring '—
    Woe's me and alas for doom's hid net!
    Yet oh, may the Right be triumphant yet!

(Mesode.)

' So gracious of heart is the Fair of Face   140
  To the strengthless cubs—soft dewdrop-things—
Of ravening lions, and loveth well
  The tender younglings that crave the udder
Of all the children of field and fell:
Therefore she saith, " Zeus, do me a grace:
  Avenge me of these my fosterlings!"

Yon eagle-omen in part then brings
Good—yet hath it somewhat whereat I shudder.
To Apollo the Healer-god I cry;
　I beseech him to plead with the Huntress, that she
　Send no blasts breathing adversely
To cause the Danaan galleys to lie　　　　　150
Harbour-bound while the months go by,
To force them to offer a sacrifice dread,
Strange, lawless, whereof no feast is spread,
The seed of a feud that shall cleave to the house,
That begetteth rebellion against a spouse:
For therein doth a haunting curse remain,
　The treacherous wrath that forgetteth never,
　Though in seeming suppressed, re-arising ever,
Set on revenge for the child that was slain.'
　Such doom, albeit with blessings blent,
Did Kalchas' voice shriek forth to the kings
　From the omen seen in the way as they went,
And my voice with the boding in consonance rings—
　　Woe's me and alas for doom's hid net !
　　Yet oh, may the Right be triumphant yet !
　　　　　　　　　(Str. 2)

Zeus—whate'er ' Zeus' expresseth of His essence—
　If the name please him on the lips of prayer, [160
With this name on my lips I seek his presence,
　Knowing none else I may with him compare.

Yea, though I ponder, in the balance laying
　All else, no help save Zeus alone I find,
If I would cast aside the burden weighing,
　All to no profit, ever on my mind.
　　　　　　　　　(Ant. 2)

He that erstwhile was lord of all created,
　Set in resistless battle-might on high,

Now shall none name him, the oblivion-fated,
  Seeing his day is utterly gone by.   170

Yea, his successor, from the empyrean
  Hurled by a mightier wrestler, is no more:
But whoso chanteth Zeus's triumph-pæan
  Loyally, he shall gain all wisdom's store.

                      (Str. 3)
Zeus unto men the path of wisdom showeth:
  This as the law of life doth he ordain—
' From suffering's root the flower instruction groweth.'
  Yet even in sleep the heart sees only pain

Dropping from memory's winepress: still is given
  Wisdom to scholars loth to understand: 180
The Gods from thrones of majesty in heaven
  Must force their boon into the unwilling hand.

                      (Ant. 3)
So was it then: that elder squadron-leader
  Blamed not the prophet's counsel of despair,
All helmless driven by Fate the tempest-speeder,
  What time in evil case the Achaians were,

Camped idly on the shore toward Chalkis facing,
  Whence none could sail, a-hungered, thirst-dis-
      tressed,
There where the tides this way and that way racing 190
  Past Aulis' mountain-haven, know no rest.

                      (Str. 4)
Blasts from the bitter north blew ever, bearing
  Deadly delay and famine in their train,
Havenless wanderings to and fro; unsparing
  They battered hulls, and hawsers snapped in twain;

They made the long days longer : heavy-wearing
  Hours cankered Argos' flower with idleness :—
When lo, a prophet-voice pealed out, declaring
  A cure worse than the bitter weather's stress :   200

Prophet to king spake, challenging defiance
  Of Artemis' decree : then horror-thrilled
Dashed to the ground their sceptres Atreus' scions,
  And with indignant tears their eyes were filled.

                          (Ant. 4)

In dark despair the elder King spake, crying,
  ' Woe to me if I do not her command !
Yet oh, to see mine house's darling lying
  Upon the altar, and upon mine hand
The life-streams of a slaughtered maiden dyeing   210
  A father's fingers !—wretched choice for me !
Yet—how forsake the ships, like recreant flying ?
  How forfeit all this great confederacy ?

None may blame these whose clamour fury-laden
  Demands a sacrifice to lull to rest
The winds, though nought save slaughter of a maiden
  Avail—ah me ! may all be for the best ! '

                          (Str. 5)

So he stooped 'neath the yoke of fate's compulsion ;
And the godless blast of a spirit's revulsion
  Swept through him, unclean, unhallowed, turning 220
His soul to a purpose of reckless daring :—
Oh hideous wellspring of woes, the uncaring
  Frenzy that trampleth on honour, the burning
Passion that steels hearts !   Thus the severance
Of the fetter that trammelled the fleet, the deliverance
  Of a wanton was he by his child's blood earning !

(Ant. 5)

And the child-voice crying 'O father!' and pleading
Those battle-fain deemsters heard unheeding;   230
   But her father, so soon as the prayer had been
     chanted,
Bade the ministers raise her—yea, bade none falter—
Like a kid, all drooping, above the altar
   Close-swathed in her vesture; and, even as panted
Her lovely lips with the words outrushing,
Bade stay with the curb's might utterance-crushing
   The curse, lest his house thereby should be haunted.

(Str. 6)

And, with saffron-dyed robes to the earth down-stream-
     ing,
Each death-priest she smote with the shaft pity-
     gleaming   240
   Of her glance—as a picture with eyes imploring
That seemeth in act to speak—to soften
Those hearts of stone!   Ah, often and often
   Had her sire's halls thrilled to the glad outpouring
Of her song by the tables banquet-laden,
When the wine-drops were spilled, and the pure-
     voiced maiden
   Called down Heaven's blessing in chants adoring.

(Ant. 6)

And then—O, I saw not, I tell not!   Fair issue
Had Kalchas' devisings!   The fateful tissue
   Of instruction from Justice's loom down-sweepeth
On such as have suffered :—but what is her dooming
Suffice it to know in the day of its coming.   [250
   Who knoweth beforehand, beforehand weepeth.
With the dawn's forthshining shall come revelation.

That the end may be well is the supplication
  Of the near one, the dear one, who this land keepeth.

Enter Klytemnestra.

Queen, reverencing thy majesty I come ;
For meet it is to honour the King's wife,
When of its lord the throne stands tenantless.   260
But whether for good tidings heard or no
With hopes that herald joy thou sacrifice
Fain would I hear, yet grudge not reticence.

KLYTEMNESTRA.

' With heralding of good,' as saith the saw,
' Forth let the Dawn break from her mother Night.'
A joy beyond hope's vision shalt thou learn :
For Priam's city have the Argives ta'en.

CHORUS.

What said'st thou ?—through unfaith it 'scaped my
    ear.

KLYTEMNESTRA.

The Achaians hold Troy : speak I clearly now ?

CHORUS.

Joy thrills me, crying challenge to my tears !   270

KLYTEMNESTRA.

Thy loyalty in thy visage stands confest.

CHORUS.

Now hast thou token sure thereof ?—and what ?

KLYTEMNESTRA.

I have—how not ?—except a god delude.

CHORUS.

Dost thou lend easy credence to dream-shows?

KLYTEMNESTRA.

Not for me fantasies of slumbering sense!

CHORUS.

Hath then some wingless rumour gladdened thee?

KLYTEMNESTRA.

As some young girl's hast thou misprized my wit!

CHORUS.

How long time is it since the city fell?

KLYTEMNESTRA.

Even in the night that gave this dayspring birth.

CHORUS.

What messenger to such speed could attain?   280

KLYTEMNESTRA.

The Fire-god :—he from Ida splendour hurled.
Beacon to beacon flung the courier-flame
Hitherward.   Ida gleamed to Hermes' crag
In Lemnos.   From the isle that giant torch
Did Athos third, the scaur of Zeus, receive.
Soaring o'er flame-lit ridges of the sea
That torch triumphant journeying in his strength,
The pine's gold-gleaming splendour, like a sun,
Passed to Makistus' heights its message on :
Nor loitering he, nor heedless, as by sleep   290
O'ermastered, failed his part in heralding :
But o'er Euripus' flood the beacon-gleam
Far-flying brought Messapius' watchmen word.

They flashed back answer, sped the tidings on,
Touching with fire a heath-pile sapless-old.
The Titan torch in yet unminished might
High leaping o'er Asopus' plain—it seemed
A bright moon rising—to Kithairon's crag,
Uproused a new relay of courier-fire.
And there the watch disowned it not, the light   300
Far sent, but lit a huger bale than all.
And the glare darted o'er Gorgopis' mere,
And, winning unto Aigiplanktos' hill,
Bade, ' Stint not ye the ordinance of fire ! '
Uptossed they, kindled in unscanted might,
A giant beard of flame that glaring soared
Over the foreland that on Saron's firth
Looks : down it lightened then, until it won
Arachnê's watchtower-steeps hard by our town.
Thence to the Atreids' palace down it flashed,   310
This far-descended child of Ida's fire.
Thus they which ran my torch-race by such rule,
Hand passing it on to hand, fulfilled their course ;
Victor the first is, though he raceth last.
Such sign, such token, tell I unto thee
Of tidings sent me by my lord from Troy.

CHORUS.

Hereafter will I thank the Gods, O Queen :
Now would I fain hear once again throughout,
And marvel at the story thou dost tell.

KLYTEMNESTRA.

Masters of Troy this day the Achaians are.   320
Discordant cries, I ween, are loud therein.
Pour into one bowl vinegar and oil—

These shalt thou name antagonists, not friends;
So from the vanquished and the victors now
Are diverse cries heard, born of diverse plight.
These, fallen on the bodies of their slain—
On husband, brother, yea, on grey-haired sire
The children—o'er the doom of dear, dear dead,
With lips that now are slaves' lips wail aloud.
Those—toil of vigil and fight constraineth them   330
Famished to break their fast on what the town
Hath ready, in no order billeted :
But, even as each hath drawn the lot of chance,
In Trojan mansions, now the spoil of spears,
They lodge this day, escaped the frosts and dews
Of naked skies, and careless as the Gods
Shall sleep the livelong night unsentinelled.
If these respect the Gods that in the land
Made captive dwell, and temples of the Gods,
The smiters shall not in their turn be smitten.   340
But may no lust of greed upon the host
Descend, for rapine of forefended things.
For yet remains their half-race, even to run
The backward course in scatheless home-return.
Yea, though in heaven's sight guiltless fare the host
Homeward, for slaughtered victims vengeance still
Might wake—ay, though no sudden ills befall.
Lo, this thou hear'st from mine, a woman's mouth.
Now, in no doubtful balance, triumph the right !
This boon above all blessings do I choose.   350

Chorus.

Queen, like a wise man's, gracious is thy speech.
I, hearing the sure token named of thee,

Address me to thanksgiving to the Gods.
For priceless meed of labour hath been won.
> [*Exit Klytemnestra.*

Hail to thee, Zeus, O King!   Hail, night of joy,
   Winner for us of glory, who hast flung
A net close-trammelling o'er the towers of Troy!
   Ha, none may overleap, nor old nor young,
Ruin's all-snaring coil that makes them thraldom's
     spoil,   [360
   Whose mighty meshes round their lives have clung!

Worship and thanks to Zeus who wards the right
   Of host and guest!   On Paris did he strain
Long since his bow, that his true shaft might light
Not ere the appointed hour, nor waste its flight
   In voids beyond the stars, sped all in vain.
                     (Str. 1)

   They have for their transgression's meed
     The stroke of Zeus: his hand herein
     All men may trace: who wrought the sin
   Have suffered as He hath decreed.

   Who dares aver the Gods reck nought   370
     Of human actions when man flings
     The sanctity of holy things
   Beneath his feet?—an impious thought!

   Now stands revealed the vengeance reaped
     When bold presumption, in despite
     Of Justice, breathes the rage of fight
   In pride of wealth by wrong upheaped.

   But O, be mine a lot kept free
     From suffering: mine be feet that pace

Paths that the steps of wisdom trace:
So shall content companion me.   380

For riches shall be no defence
  Unto the man who from his sight
  Spurns the great altar of the Right
In pride of full-fed insolence.

(Ant. 1)

Yet is man haled as with a chain,
  By scheming Ruin's resistless child,
  Temptation, into sin beguiled.
What cure avails?—all, all are vain!

Not hidden is the mischief: nay,
  The gleam thereof glares lurid-dyed,
  And, like bronze tempered ill, when tried   390
By touchstone-rasp and blows' assay,

So shows the sinner black in grain.
  He chases, like some child, the wings
  Elusive of a bird, and brings
Upon his country hopeless bane;

And no God heareth when he prays:
  Nay, but the very God to whom
  He kneeleth, spurns him to his doom
Who walketh in injustice' ways.

Even such was Paris: to the home   400
  Of Atreus' royal sons he came,
  And heaped on that guest-table shame,
In that he stole the wife therefrom.

(Str. 2)

And she left to her people the spear-clang ringing
  On shields, and the arming of war-hosts sent

Overseas ; and to Ilium for dowry bringing
  Ruin, through those gates swiftly she went :—
Such a horror she dared! And, with groans proclaiming
  Their grief, did the seers of her house lament :
‘ Woe for the home, for the rulers' shaming,   410
  For Love's lost footprints, his bow unbent ! ’
But he—he is silent, is unreviling,
  Though the world hath beheld him the scorned, the
      forsaken :
Overseas is his heart ; and a phantom, beguiling
  His spirit, her place in his palace hath taken :
  And statues of loveliest mould may waken
    Loathing alone ; in his famishing eyes
    Each spell of the Love-queen shattered lies.

                    (Ant. 2)

Vain joys in slumber a ravishing vision   420
  Brings to the heart that doth wake and weep.
He seeth in fancy a rapture Elysian,
  And his arms enclasp it, but may not keep.
Vanished the vision is, unreturning,
  On wings that follow the paths of sleep.
In such anguished bereavement that house is yearning :
  Yea, and bitterer harvest than this shall it reap.
And all through Hellas for heroes departed
  Love widowed, love orphaned, in desolate places
Is waiting, unknowing and patient-hearted :   430
  Yet shall anguish of mockery fill their embraces ;
  For, instead of the unforgotten faces
    Of the heroes they dream of, to each man's home
    Armour and ashes—nought else—shall come.

                    (Str. 3)

    The War-god, who exchangeth
      Men's lives for gold,

And, where the mad spear rangeth,
  The scales doth hold,
Sends back to hearts that yearn
For a brave man's return,   440
Filling one small sad urn
  Pyre-ashes cold.

With sighs love tells their story :—
  In battle bold
Was one : one fell with glory
  With garments rolled
In blood :—and each man died
All for another's bride !
In whispered pain and pride
  Is the tale told.

While here grief's hushed defiance   450
  Chides bitter-souled
Atreus' avenging scions,
  There, lapped in mould,
They, round the embattled steep,
In death yet comely, sleep ;
The land they won —and keep—
  Doth these enfold.

                                    (Ant. 3)

A people's execration
  Speaks stern and low,
As when an outraged nation
  Curses her foe.
Ah me ! mine heart is fain
For what comes in night's train !   460
Slayers of many slain
  Gods watch, I trow.

Unrighteous gain but tendeth
　　To overthrow.
The dark Erinnys endeth
　　All at one blow :
Then is the proud down thrust
To darkness and to dust,
There where the strengthless must
　　All hope forego.

Fame above measure given
　　Brings man but woe :
Full in his eyes Zeus' levin
　　Flasheth its glow.　　　　　　　　470
Let mine unenvied weal
Nor crush with armèd heel
Cities, nor conquest feel,
　　Nor thraldom know.

Tidings on flaming wings of triumph flew,
　　And swift through Argos goes
The rumour of it : yet if all be true,
Or if 'tis some heaven-sent delusion—who,
　　Ah me, who knows ?
Who is so babe-like, who in wit so maimed,
　　That all his heart should glow　　　　480
At beacon-fires that forth their message flamed,
Then, when the tale is changed, downcast and shamed,
　　Should be brought low ?
How like the woman's spirit, to be crying
　　' Hail ! ' to a boon, ere proof appear,
With eager credence past all bounds swift-flying!
Ah, but the rumour woman-vouched swift-dying
　　Fails from the cheated ear.

Soon shall we prove the faith of cresset-glare
And beacon, and the swift relays of fire,   490
If true they were, or whether, false as dreams,
That welcome light came but to cheat our hearts.
Lo, from the beach a herald comes, his brows
Wreathed with the olive-sprays.   Yon dust he bears,
Twin-sister of the mire, my witness is
That no dumb tongue—not like thy kindled flame
Of mountain-logs, and smoke—shall now tell all:
But, either words shall fuller joy proclaim,
Or—out upon aught that contraveneth this!
Come sequel glad to that glad vision seen!   500
Whoso for this land prayeth otherwise,
His harvest be the sin of his own soul!

Enter Herald.

HERALD.

All hail, ancestral soil of Argive land!
As dawns the tenth year unto thee I come.
This one of many wrecked hopes wins to port.
Never I trusted even here to die
And share a dear grave in the Argive land.
All hail, O land! light of the sun, all hail!
Hail, Zeus high-throned o'er Argos! Pythian King,
Thy bow upon us rain its shafts no more!   510
Suffice that vengeance by Skamander-stream:
Now turn thou, Saviour be, be Healer, King
Apollo!   To all Gods of Festival
I cry, and to my champion Hermes cry,
Dear Herald-god, of heralds aye adored.
Heroes, who sped us forth, O welcome home
Graciously us, the remnant 'scaped the spear!

Hail, halls of kings, hail, roof-tree well-beloved,
Hail, shrines revered, and Gods that take the morning !
If ever of old, so now, with love-lit eyes   520
With honour greet our King who comes so late.
For bringing light in darkness is he come
To you and all these—Agamemnon King !
O greet him well—'tis seemly so to do—
Who with the mattock of avenging Zeus
Hath dug down Troy, hath ploughed up all her plain.
Vanished her altars are, her fanes of Gods ;
All the land's seed hath perished utterly.
Such yoke upon the neck of Troy was cast
By Atreus' elder son, the King, who comes   530
Heaven-blest, most worship-worthy of living men ;
Since Paris nor his crime-abettor, Troy,   ·
Can boast the penalty matched not the deed.
He, of abduction and of theft convict,
Forfeit hath paid, hath mown in ruin down
His father's house, his fatherland withal.
Twofold hath Priam's line for trespass paid.

CHORUS.

Glad greeting, herald from Achaia's host !

HERALD.

Glad ?—though I died now, I would murmur not !

CHORUS.

Did love of home so wrestle with thine heart ?   540

HERALD.

So much, mine eyes are dim with happy tears.

CHORUS.

Some sweetness was there in your heart-ache, then.

HERALD.

How ?—teach me, so that I may grasp thy drift.

CHORUS.

Hearts yearned at home for you who yearned for them.

HERALD.

Ha ! the land sickened for her homesick host ?

CHORUS.

Ay, from a darkened spirit oft I groaned.

HERALD.

Why brooded o'er your hearts this dire despair ?

CHORUS.

Silence, long since I proved, is wrong's one salve.

HERALD.

Afraid wast thou—of whom, thy King afar ?

CHORUS.

Ay,—as thou saidst, content I now would die.   550

HERALD.

Yea, all is well.   Yet, in that weary time,
Albeit I could tell of much fair speed,
Some hardships vexed us :—who, except the Gods,
Lives sorrowless in all things evermore ?
Of travail might I tell, bleak bivouac,
Of iron-bound coasts, hard lying, groans on groans—
Who knows how many ?—through the straitened days.
Then came new ills on land to vex us more :
Hard by our foes' walls through the nights we lay ;
And dews from heaven, and reek of marshy mead 560

Down drizzled, clammy-cleaving, rotting vest,
And making man's hair like a wild beast's fell.
But O to tell of winters that slew birds,
By snows of Ida made intolerable,
Of heats, when on his midnoon couch the sea
Unrippled sank and slept, and no breath stirred !
What boots to grieve o'er these ? Our toils are past—
Ay, from our dead hath utterly past away
All care, though it were but to rise again !
Why of those wasted lives take nice account ?   570
Why need the living grieve for adverse fate ?
I to disaster bid a long farewell.
For us, the remnant of the Argive host,
The gain outweighs, the suffering strikes the beam ;
So that we well may boast to yonder sun,
As over sea and over land we fleet—
' The Argive army, conquerors of Troy,
Hang up these spoils, a glory to their Gods,
In ancient sanctuaries all Hellas through.'
Now that ye hear this, Argos and her chiefs   580
Ought ye to praise. The grace of Zeus, which wrought
This, shall have honour.   Thou hast all my tale.

CHORUS.

Thou hast routed my misgivings ; this I own.
'Tis ne'er too late for old men to learn good.
Yet this, as meet is, toucheth most the Queen
And the House Royal : I too am rich therein.

Enter Klytemnestra.

KLYTEMNESTRA.

Erewhile I raised the jubilation-shout
When came the first night-messenger of fire

Telling Troy's capture and her overthrow.
And one spake chiding, ' Unto beacon-tenders   590
Givest thou credence, to think Troy is sacked ?
True woman thou, whose heart for such cause leaps ! '
So was I made to seem delusion's fool.
Yet sacrificed I : by thy queen's decree
One from another caught up jubilant cries
Through Argos, while in temples of the Gods
They lulled with wine the odorous incense-flame.
And now, what need that more thou tell to me ?
Of my lord's self will I learn all the tale.
Haste will I now, with honour to receive   600
My lord revered at his home-coming.   What
Can dawn with sweeter light to wife than this
The day she flings wide doors to her lord brought safe
By God from war ?   Thou tell mine husband this,
To come with all speed, come, the land's desire—
To come and find a leal wife in his halls,
Even as he left her, as a watch-dog staunch
To guard his home, a foe unto his foes,
And in all else the same, who of his seals
Have broken not one all this weary while.   610
Pleasure with man beside, or rumoured shame
No more I know than—how to dye a sword.

[Exit.

HERALD.

Such protest proud, with truth fraught, misbeseems
No high-born lady's lips to utter forth.

CHORUS.

So hath she spoken, so thou hear'st a tale
Fair-seeming—to clear-eyed interpreters.

Speak, herald—I of Menelaus ask:
Hath he, from perils safe brought back, returned,
And come with you, this land's belovèd prince ?

HERALD.

I cannot tell things false and fair to hear,   620
So that my friends should long reap fruit of joy.

CHORUS.

Would God thou couldst both tell good news and true !
'Tis all too plain that they be severed here.

HERALD.

Lost is the hero from Achaia's host,
He and his galley : truth is this I tell.

CHORUS.

Lost ?—when in sight of friends he sailed from Troy ?—
Or swept away by a storm that vexed ye all ?

HERALD.

Like perfect archer hast thou hit the mark,
And long calamity hast summed in brief.

CHORUS.

Hath rumour come from any mariners   630
Beside, that speaks him living yet or dead ?

HERALD.

None knoweth, to give clear report thereof,
Except the sun, who fostereth all the earth.

CHORUS.

How, say'st thou, came that tempest on the host,
By the Gods' anger, and how ended it ?

HERALD.

With an ill tale to mar thanksgiving's day
Fits not.   Heaven's praise should rest inviolate.
Now when with clouded brow a herald brings
Hideous disaster from a field of rout,
And speaks a nation stricken with one wound,   640
Speaks many a light of many a home doom-banned
By Arês' twy-lashed scourge of fire and steel—
Twin slaughter-curse, blood-boultered chariot-pair,—
Yea, when one cometh burdened with such woes,
Well may he chant such pæan-hymn of fiends.
But when a herald of deliverance
Comes to a town exulting in her weal—
How shall I mingle good with evil, tell
Of storm that spake to Greeks the wrath of Gods?
For they which heretofore were utter foes,   650
Even Fire and Sea, conspired and plighted faith
For havoc of the Argives' hapless host.
One night a ruin of stormy billows surged :
Galley on galley by the norland blasts
Was hurled: adrift with helpless-plunging prows
Before the whirlwind storm, the rain of spray,
Vanished they, sheep by a demon shepherd chased.
And when uprose the sun's clear light, we saw
The Aegæan Sea, a field of death, whose flowers
Were corpses of Achaians, wrecks of ships.   660
Ourselves and our good ship's unshattered hull
Some God, no man, whose hand was on our helm,
From doom snatched, or by intercession saved.
Fortune the Saviour sat and steered the bark,
That not at anchor riding was she swamped,
Nor crashed her keel upon the iron-bound shore.

Then, having 'scaped the Hades of the sea,
In clear day, doubtful of our own good hap,
Over this new disaster brooded we
Of the host stricken, beaten small as dust.   670
And now, if any of those be breathing yet,
Of us they speak as perished men—how not?—
As in like manner account we of their plight.
Yet may the best befall!   For Menelaus,
With fullest hope look for him first to come.
Yea, if the sun's rays know him yet alive
And seeing light, by some device of Zeus,
Who wills not yet to annihilate his line,
Hope is there that he shall win home again.
All hast thou heard; and, know, thou hast heard
   truth.   680
                             [*Exit.*

Chorus.   (*Str.* 1)

   Now who was it named her so
      With such a prophetic name?
        Was it one whom we may not see?
Did the All-foreknowing her doom foreshow
   Through the tongue that foreshadowed her evil
      fame,
     And named her Helen, that she should be
     Spear-wooed, and a kindler of enmity?
       Helen?—nay, but a Hell—
       Read we the riddle well—
To the ships, to the heroes, the town, that for her sake
   fell.
She fled from the delicate-costly hangings veiling 690
Her couch, on the breath of the Titan West-wind
   sailing:

But shielded hunters, a warrior host, were chasing
Her flight on the printless track of the oars swift-
    racing,
  Till there, where the forest mantles Simois' strand,
  For the blood-stained strife they drave their keels
    a-land.

(Ant. 1)

    By relentless Wrath was she brought
      Unto Ilium—*dear* indeed !—   700
      By the Wrath that avenged the wrong
  That her sin to the board of the guest had wrought,
    And to Zeus, of the guest-bond who taketh heed.
     Ay, the vengeance came, though it tarried long,
     On the vaunting chant of the festal throng,
      Even the bridal lay
     Which the bridegroom's kin that day
Sang to the glory of him who had borne her away.
But the ancient city of Priam in dust repenting   710
Is learning the dirge of a multitude's lamenting :
Yea, and I ween in this hour with bitter sighing
' Out upon Paris, the bridegroom of Death ! ' is she
    crying
  Mid the dirge for the blood of her sons that her
    multitude raise ;
  For the dregs hath she drained of a cup of ruinous
    days.

(Str. 2)

    It was even as when one keepeth
     A lion-whelp in his home
     Yet craving the teat wherefrom
    It was stolen ; in young life's dawning   720
    Tame, with the children it leapeth :
     'Tis a joy in the elders' eyes,

And oft in their arms' warm nest
Like a nursling infant it lies,
Bright-eyed for caressing, and fawning
At hunger's imperious hest.

(Ant. 2)

But, older grown, it displayeth
  The inherited lion-strain ;
  For it rendeth the sheep it hath slain,
In requital for nurture : unbidden   730
That feaster his banquet arrayeth,
  And blood-defiled is the house.
    From its fury the scared slaves quail,
  From the horror murderous
'Neath that roof for its ruin long hidden,
  A god-sent priest of bale.

(Str. 3)

Even so on Ilium-town
Floated a spirit down
  Of peace, by seeming,
Of windless peace, a crown   740
Over her wealth-renown
  Soft splendour beaming ;
An arrow of desire
  That archer-eyes were winging ;
  A flower soul-thrilling, springing
Out of love's bed of fire.
Yet from all this she turned : a bitter ending
  For all that promised bridal bliss she wrought,
That fatal sojourner and guest descending
  On Priam's line, a Fury ruin-fraught
  From Guest-ward Zeus, tears to their house she
    brought.

(Ant. 3)

> A saying of old—once known   750
> Of all for wisdom's own—
>   Thus to men crieth:
> ' Great weal to fulness grown
> Reaps even as it hath sown,
>   Nor childless dieth;
> But fair prosperity
>   Aye bears for man one fated
>   Child of her womb, the unsated
> Vampire Misery.'

But I alone stand, holding, as none other,
   That Sin it is, the godless *act*, that bears
Spawn like itself, foul offspring of foul mother: 760
   But they whose straight path righteousness prepares,
   Fair is their lot, and goodly issue theirs.

(Str. 4)

> But Arrogance, in sin grown grey
>   Mid vile men, bears a child at length
>   Like her in name, in lusty strength,
> Or soon or late, when dawns her day;

> Yea, and a brother-fiend, whom none
>   May cope with, impious Hardihood—
>   Black curses twain o'er homes that brood, 770
> And like their dam each demon son.

(Ant. 4)

> In smoke-fouled huts doth Justice shine;
>   On virtuous lives she still hath smiled:
>   From gold-tricked halls and hands defiled,
> She turns her with averted eyne.

> A guest she is of each pure soul:
>   She on the power of wealth looks down,

With all its base coin of renown: 780
She guideth all things to their goal.

Enter Agamemnon in a chariot with Kassandra.

Hail to the King who hath laid Troy low
    In the dust!   Hail, Atreus' seed!
How shall I greet thee?   How shall I show
    Reverence due, that the meed
Of thy welcome be not overshot by the bow,
    Be not under-run by the steed?
For many of mortals honour, in sooth,
Mere semblance, setting at nought heart's truth.
Ay, ready be all to bear their part
In bemoaning the stricken—but sorrow's dart   790
Hath left them unscathed; it hath pierced not the
    heart.
They rejoice in thy joy—but their gladness is feigned,
For the smileless lips are to smiles constrained.
But a shepherd of folk who is shrewd to discern
Shall nowise be cheated by eyes that shine
Soft as from hearts that in loyalty yearn,
While their love is to true love as water to wine.

But thou, what time yon war-host was arrayed
    For Helen's sake— I will hide nought!—   800
Wast with no flattering portraiture portrayed
    Of me: by thee the helm of thought
Was, so deemed I, that day in folly swayed,
    When thou by sacrifice hadst brought
Back courage unto men of death afraid.
But now from mine heart's depth all lovingly
    The breeze of loyalty doth blow

To meet thy triumph : thou at last shalt see,
     By inquisition made shalt know,
Who righteously, and who in perfidy
     Hath ruled thy folk for thee.

AGAMEMNON.

First, Argos and the Gods of fatherland   810
I greet, as right is—Gods who wrought with me
Mine home-return and that great vengeance done
On Priam's town.   The cause no human tongue
Pleaded, they heard ; and into War's red urn
Cast votes for Ilium's sack by warrior-toil
With one accord.   Unto acquittal's vase,
Came hope of votes alone—unfilled it stood.
To Ilium's fall yet witnesseth the smoke :
Still Atê's flame-blasts live there.   Dying down
Her ashes spicy-odoured breathe of wealth.   820
For this we owe the high Gods gratitude
Unfading, seeing the toils of vengeance' net
Round her were staked by us : for a woman's sake
Stamped flat their town was by the monster Horse
That Argos foaled, fraught with its shield-array,
Which leapt their walls what time the Pleiads set,
When that raw-ravening lion o'er their towers
Bounding, of blood of princes lapped his fill.
This, for unscanted prelude to the Gods :—
The thought thou spakest heard I, nor forget.   830
As thine my words are, and my heart as thine.
Full few be they in whom there lives inborn
Unenvious honour of a prosperous friend.
Venom of malice deeply taints the heart,
Doubling the burden of a soul diseased
That bends 'neath its own trouble not alone,

But sighs to see a neighbour's happiness.
I speak that I do know ; I have learnt to appraise
The mockery-friendship—phantom of a shadow—
Of men who feigned firm loyalty to me.   840
Only Odysseus, loth albeit he sailed,
Was my one never-failing yokefellow.
Of him I say this, whether he be dead
Or living.   Touching Argos and the Gods,
A general assembly will we call,
And there take counsel.   And we will devise
How what is well shall long continue so,
And, whatsoever needeth healing salves,
By searing brand or knife, in cruelty kind
Will we essay to medicine the disease.   850
Now to the halls and hallowed hearths of home
I pass ; there will I first salute the Gods
Which sent me forth and have brought home again.
Triumph attended me ; may it abide.

Enter Klytemnestra.

KLYTEMNESTRA.

Citizens, Argive ancients here in place,
I will not shame before you to confess
My wifely love.   Time makes the fear of man
To fade away.   Not lessoned by the lips
Of others, will I tell my weary life
Through long years while my lord beleaguered Troy.
First, that the wife sit from her lord afar   [860
Lone in the house, is sore calamity ;
To hear heart-shaking rumours many an one—
That this man come and that, with tales of woe
Each worse than other, crying them to the house.

Yea, if my lord had gotten as many wounds
As many-channelled rills of rumour told,
More than a net, as say they, were he pierced.
Had he, as tale on tale affirmed, so died,
He might, a second Geryon triple-framed,   870
Boast he had gotten threefold vest of earth
[Heaped o'er him—nought I say of all beneath,—][1]
Who in each several form one death had died.
By reason of these heart-shaking rumours, oft
By force did others seize me, and unknit
Rafter-hung nooses clinging round my neck.
Yea, and our son for this cause stands not here,
The warden of our troth-plight, mine and thine,
Orestes, as was meet : yet marvel not.
Fostered he is by Strophius, Phokis' king,   880
Our leal war-helper, who of twofold scathe
Forewarned me—peril unto thee by Troy,
And peril of clamorous rabble-mutiny
Hurling the council down.   Inborn in men
That proneness is, to trample on the fallen.
Think not deceit is lurking 'neath my plea !
Ay me ! the gushing fountains of my tears
Are dried up now ; no drop upwells therefrom ;
And marred with nightlong vigils are mine eyes,
While for thy sake 1 wept the beacon-piles   890
Unkindled still.   And ever midst my dreams
The light wing of the slumbrous-humming gnat
Brake off my sleep, while whelming thee I saw
More woes than could be in that slumber's space.
Now slips my load off ; now with sorrowless soul
I hail my lord as dog that wards a fold—

1.   A line rejected by good critics as spurious.

Sure mainstay of a ship—firm-stablished pillar
Of some high roof—a father's only son—
Land sighted past all hope by mariners—
Light of a fair, fair dayspring after storm—   900
Upwelling rill to thirsty wayfarer—
Oh sweet to 'scape from fear's long tyrannous strain!
Lo, with such greetings dare I honour him.
Gods, be not jealous!—sorrow's measure heaped
We have borne already.   Now, beloved lord,
Step from this car, yet set not on the ground
The foot that trampled Troy to ruin-heaps.
Handmaids, why tarry ye, whose task it is
To spread with woven splendour all his way?
His path be straightway purple-paved, that Justice 910
To a home may lead him he scarce looked to see.
As for the rest—care, never lulled to sleep,
Justly shall order fate's work, Heaven to help.

AGAMEMNON.

Daughter of Leda, warder of mine halls,
With my long absence well thy speech accords,
So long drawn out!   But fitting praise and just
From other lips must come, and not from thine.
For this thing, pamper not in woman-wise
Me, nor, like prostrate slave of Asian king,
Mouth unto me a grovelling outcry,   920
Nor pave with robes my path, so to provoke
Heaven's jealousy : ye thus must honour Gods.
For me to pace o'er purple braveries—
A mortal, me!—I dare not do this thing.
As man, not God, do honour unto me.
Tush, without footcloths, without tapestries,
My fame speaks loud.   To keep a sober mind

Is God's best gift.   Him happy must we name
Who wins life's end in sweet prosperity.
If thus we speed all through, I shall not fear.   930

KLYTEMNESTRA.

Ah, say not so, to cross my purpose now !

AGAMEMNON.

My purpose, know, I will not disannul.

KLYTEMNESTRA.

Through *fear* hast thou so vowed unto the Gods ?

AGAMEMNON.

I know, none better, what I have said: 'tis fixed.

KLYTEMNESTRA.

What think'st thou Priam, triumphing so, had done?

AGAMEMNON.

Sooth, *he* had paced o'er broidered webs, I trow.

KLYTEMNESTRA.

Then stand not thou in awe of blame of men.

AGAMEMNON.

Yet mighty is a people's murmuring.

KLYTEMNESTRA.

Tush ! he that is unenvied is unblest.

AGAMEMNON.

It misbeseems a woman so to strive.   940

KLYTEMNESTRA.

It well beseems the fortunate to yield.

AGAMEMNON.

How, car'st thou so for victory in this strife ?

KLYTEMNESTRA.

Yield !—nay, of free will grant me to prevail !

AGAMEMNON.

Nay then, if this thou wilt, straight let one loose
My shoes, the trampled servants of my feet.
May jealous glance of Gods not smite from far
Me on sea-purples trampling rich as these !
I shame to tread bright raiment in the dust,
Marring fair wealth and silver-purchased webs.
Thus much for this :—now graciously receive   950
This stranger-maid.   God kindly looks from far
On such as mercifully use their power :
For none consenting bows to thraldom's yoke.
She, of war-guerdons many the choice flower,
The gift of Hellas' host, with me hath come.
Now, as constrained to hearken unto thee,
Treading on purples to mine halls I pass.

KLYTEMNESTRA.

There is a sea—its well-springs who shall dry ?—
That breeds the silver-costly purple's flow
Abundant, fadeless, wherein vests be plunged.   960
Thine halls have store of such, by Heaven's grace,
      King ;
Thine house knows not what meaneth lack of aught.
Trampling of vests untold would *I* have vowed,
Had this in shrines prophetic been enjoined,
When I devised rich ransom for thy life.
For, while the root lives, foliage climbs the house

Uprearing shade against the dogstar's glare :
And thou, in coming to thy palace-hearth,
As sun-glow art that comes in winter-tide ;
And when in bitter clusters Zeus matures   970
Wine, then is quickening coolness in the house,
If but the presence of its lord be there.

(Agamemnon enters palace.)

Zeus ! Zeus Accomplisher ! fulfil my prayers !
Take thought for that thou meanest to fulfil !

(Enters palace.)

(Str. 1*)*

Chorus.

Why and O why doth this terror insistently haunting
    me still
Like a bird of black doom hover nigh to the heart
    that is boding ill ?
And a prophecy rings through the song that sings
    without bidding or guerdon
Evermore in mine ears, like a dream that no seers
    may interpret, whose burden
      No cheering courage, enthroned in sway   980
      Over my bosom, may spurn away.
Yet what is there now to be feared ?—is the time not
    long gone by
Since the anchors cast from the sterns gripped fast
    the sands of Troy,
      When thitherward hasted our sea-array ?

(Ant. 1*)*

I have looked on the home-return of my King, with
    mine eyes have I seen :
Myself am my witness—yet oh, the Avenging Spirit's
    keen

Peals as from the choir of my thoughts : no lyre rings
    there to lighten   990
The dirge of fear that no hope may cheer, no con·
    fidence brighten !
       My soul's dark presage is not for nought,
       Nor the rush of the flood of prophetic thought
That maddens my breast like a whirlpool that raves
    in its cavern-hall.
Yet not as this day I forebode, I pray, may the end
    befall,   [1000
       Not thus to fulfilment the issue be brought !

                          (Str. 2)

    His heart's desire of ease
      And of health shall no man win ;
    For his neighbour still is disease,
      And the party-wall is thin.
    And what though the bark of his fate
      With a straight course far and fast
    Speed—hidden the dark reefs wait
      Whereon it shall crash at the last.
    O yea, in their fear men fling
      The half of their wealth overboard—
    As one whirleth a stone from a sling—   1010
      To save the rest of their hoard.
    So the ship of a house, it may be,
      Though a curse have freighted it full,
    May not utterly founder, the sea
      Not swallow the woe-fraught hull :
    Yea, and not of such loss cometh dearth ;
      For by gifts of Zeus's hand,
    And by boons of the furrows of earth
      From their doors may famine be banned.

(Ant. 2)

But when once at thy feet on the ground
 Is spilt the blood of the slain,   1020
What spell-chant then shall be found
 That shall gather it up again ?
Else, wherefore did Zeus' stroke still
 In stern foreknowledge the breath
Of the Master of Healing, whose skill
 Could raise up mortals from death ?
Yet—did not a Fate, from of old
 Established supreme, restrain
Even Gods, that they cannot mould
 Always the doom they ordain—
Mine heart would outstrip my tongue,
 Would pour forth its hidden tale ;
But darkness around it is hung   1030
 For a shroud : it must wait and wail ;
And in anguish of soul, in despair
 Of unknitting the links of the chain
That is dragging my lords to the snare,
 Aflame is my spirit—in vain !

Re-enter Klytemnestra.

KLYTEMNESTRA.

Pass in thou too—Kassandra, thee I name—
Since Zeus unangerly hath made thee share
Our house's laver-rites, midst many such
Our thralls, by Zeus Wealth-warder's altar ranged.
Step from the car ; be not disdainful-souled.
What, even Alkmena's son, men say, of yore   1040
Was sold a slave, and brooked to bear the yoke.
If then such doom of fortune fall to thee,
Thank Heaven if thine be lords of ancient wealth.

They which have reaped rich harvest past their hopes
Are overmeasure alway stern to thralls:
With us thou hast all rights of use and wont.

CHORUS.

To thee she saith plain words, and so makes end.
Since toils of destiny have tangled thee,
Obey, if this thou wilt—ha! wouldst refuse!

KLYTEMNESTRA.

Nay then, except, in swallow-wise, she own　　1050
An uncouth speech of some outlandish folk,
My words must reach her wit, and must prevail.

CHORUS.

Pass in: what for thy state is best, she saith.
Obey, and leave thy seat upon the car.

KLYTEMNESTRA.

My leisure serves me not to tarry here
Without.　Beside the hearth, the home's mid-shrine,
The victims stand, and wait the knife, the fire,
For us who never hoped to win such grace.
If thou wilt do my bidding, tarry not:
But if thou understand not these my words,　　1060
In speech's stead sign with thine alien hand.

CHORUS.

'Tis an interpreter the stranger needs,
Meseems.　Her mien is wild as beast new-trapped.

KLYTEMNESTRA.

Sure she is mad, hears but her maniac thoughts,
Who hath left a city newly sacked, and come

Hither, nor yet hath learned to brook the curb,
Ere she in blood hath foamed away her rage.
I waste no more words, to be flouted so!

[Exit.

CHORUS.

I, for I pity her, will not be wroth.
Come, hapless maiden thou, avoid yon car.   1070
Consent to feel fate's yoke, unfelt before.

KASSANDRA.   (Str. 1)

Woe and alas!—alas, O Earth!
Apollo! Apollo!

CHORUS.

Wherefore for Loxias hast thou raised this cry?
No God is he for mourners' company.

KASSANDRA.   (Ant. 1)

Woe and alas!—alas, O Earth!
Apollo! Apollo!

CHORUS.

Lo, she blasphemes, invokes the God again!
It fits not he attend the wailers' strain.

KASSANDRA.   (Str. 2)

Apollo! Apollo!   1080
O Highway-god, destroyer of me!
For lightly hast thou this second time destroyed me!

CHORUS.

Lo, words of prophecy of her own ills!
Even the thrall's soul inspiration thrills.

KASSANDRA. *(Ant. 2)*

Apollo ! Apollo !
O Highway-god, destroyer of me !
Whither hast led me, to what roof convoyed me ?

CHORUS.

The Atreids' roof.   If thou to this art blind,
I tell thee : falsehood here thou shalt not find.

KASSANDRA. *(Str. 3)*

Nay, but a haunt of the haters of God, which is
    privy withal   1090
Unto manifold murders of kinsmen, to gins wherein
    doomed men fall :
Yea, 'tis a human shambles, the floor of a blood-reek-
    ing hall !

CHORUS.

Keen-scented seems the stranger, like a hound
Questing the blood-slot till the prey is found.

KASSANDRA. *(Ant. 3)*

Nay, I mistake not : the evidence yonder is plain to
    see.
There, there be the children that weep for their own
    foul butchery,
Weep for their flesh that was roasted, a feast for their
    father to be !

CHORUS.

Sooth, thy prophetic fame hath reached our ears ;
But for that ancient tale we need no seers.

KASSANDRA.　　　　(*Str. 4*)

What plotteth the plotter ?—woe and alas !　1100
　What strange dark deed in the house this day
Is devised, yea, now is coming to pass
　Unendurable, cureless, while helpers stay
　　Ah, far away !

CHORUS.

This thy last bodement's mark I cannot hit :
That know I ; all the city rings with it.

KASSANDRA.　　　　(*Ant. 4*)

Even now, O wretch, dost thou compass the deed !
　Thy lord in the bath thou refreshest—ah how,
How shall I utter the issue ?—with speed
　Shall it come !—thine hand to the blade stretchest
　　thou　　　　　　　　　　　　　1110
　　　　Even now, even now !

CHORUS.

Not yet I understand : perplexed am I
Now, after riddles, by dark prophecy.

KASSANDRA.　　　　(*Str. 5*)

Ha, horror on horror !　What yonder riseth ?—
　A net is this ?—O meshes of hell !
And the net is his wife !—his death she deviseth.
　Now let the unglutted Furies yell
O'er the sacrifice that she sacrificeth !—
　Oh, a death of stoning should guerdon it well !

CHORUS.

What, what Erinnys summonest thou to wail
This house's dirge ?—thy words have made me quail.
　Back to mine heart the ruddy life-drops run, [1120

Such drops as, in life's fated even falling,
  Beat time unto the sinking of life's sun :—
  I hear doom, swift doom, calling !

KASSANDRA.   (Ant. 5)

Ha see ! ha see !—from his mate deliver
  The bull !—her treachery-robes adorn
Him whom a victim trapped they give her ;
  And she hews down him of the sable horn.
In the brimming laver his limp limbs quiver !—
  Of the bath of murder I warn thee—I warn !

CHORUS.

In divination may I boast no skill: 1130
Yet these words, as I deem, forebode but ill.
  But—out of oracles what word of aid
Is framed for man ?   These bodings weirdly-ringing
  Come mischief-fraught to hearts that hear dismayed
    Their lessons terror-bringing.

KASSANDRA.   (Str. 6)

Woe, woe is me for the ill doom wrought upon me the
    evil-starred !—
Ay, for I moan my doom—mine own with my lord's
    fate now do I blend.
Unto what end, O lost king, hast thou brought the
    hapless hitherward ?
For nought but to be here slain with thee !—what
    other can be the end ?

CHORUS.

O frenzied heart, O demon-possessed, who touching
    thyself hast chanted   1140

E

A tuneless strain, like the sad refrain of the nightingale tawny-golden
Who for Itys, Itys, with burdened breast, with spirit
  misery-haunted
Wails on and on, while the long days run of a life
  with woes enfolden.

KASSANDRA.   *(Ant. 6)*

Ah me, that the doom of the nightingale clear-voiced
  mine own might be!
For in plume and wing soft-compassing the Gods her
  body arrayed;
And her life-days pass like a pleasant tale, and from
  tears of sorrow free.
But for me doth wait a merciless fate—the stroke of
  the two-edged blade!

CHORUS.

Ah whence be the god-given visions that crowd on
  thee, horrors rashly boded?   1150
This tale thou hast told hast thou shaped in the mould
  of song where is death's voice crying!
Thine ominous strains are shrilling loud with an
  utterance terror-loaded.
Where be they found, the limits that bound the paths
  of thy weird prophesying?

KASSANDRA.   *(Str. 7)*

Woe for the wedlock of Paris, for all whom he loved
  ruin-laden!
  Woe for Skamander, the stream that our fathers
  knew!

Once, once on thy margent nurtured, a misery-fated
    maiden,
        To womanhood I grew.
Now on the brink of the River of Wailing, the Stream
    of Despair,   1160
'Neath the imminent darkness I shiver : my prophecy-
    chant ends there!

CHORUS.

What thing hast thou uttered ?—too plain for mistak-
    ing!
  To a babe that had heard it its import were clear.
As a stab my heart felt it—mine heart is aching
For thy bitterest doom, for thine heart that is breaking
      'Neath horrors I pale to hear.

KASSANDRA.   (Ant. 7)

Woe for the city through long-drawn agonies ruinward
    reeling!
  Woe for the altars whereon my sire offered up
Pastureland-nurslings by hecatombs, yet no salve of
    healing
        Dropped thence in the deadly cup   1170
Troy drank : there was no returning from death's
    door, none that would save!
And I—full soon shall my burning heart be stilled in
    the grave.

CHORUS.

'Tis the same song still from thy lips outrushing!
  A malignant God is constraining thee,
Descending upon thee with might soul-crushing,
That the wine of death from thy spirit is gushing.
    But the end—oh, what shall it be?

KASSANDRA.

Nay then, no more the oracle through veils
Shall shyly peer, like some new-wedded bride;
But cloudless-clear to sunriseward, I wot,   1180
Its wind shall blow, till, like a crashing surge,
Flash to the light a mightier woe than all.
No more by riddles will I lesson you:
Ye, coursing with me, witness how I scent
The slot of evil deeds wrought long ago.
List—never leaves yon roof that chorus-crew
Whose harmony is discord—a curse-chant.
They have lapped up human blood; so, bolder grown,
Aye haunt the house that hellish revel-rout
Whose presence none may ban, the Sister Fiends.1190
There brooding o'er the halls they chant their hymn,
The Primal Curse, anon spit loathing on
The Brother's Bed which ruined its defiler.[1]
Ha, have I missed, or shot like archer true?
'Prophet of lies' am I, and 'street-door babbler'?
First take thou oath, then witness that I know,
Untaught, this house's sins of long ago.

CHORUS.

Nay, how should oath-plight in all honour given
Bring healing here?   Yet marvel I that thou,
Nursed oversea, should of an alien town   1200
Speak, and speak sooth, as one that dwelt therein.

KASSANDRA.

Prophet Apollo made this office mine.

---

1. Alluding to the adultery of Thyestes with Aeropê, wife of
his brother Atreus.

CHORUS.

A God—yet smitten with desire of thee!

KASSANDRA.

I shamed to speak of this tale heretofore.

CHORUS.

Ay, with prosperity goes ever pride.

KASSANDRA.

A fervent suitor he, who breathed fierce love.

CHORUS.

Came ye together by love's ordinance?

KASSANDRA.

I promised Loxias—then I broke my troth.

CHORUS.

His boon already given of prophecy?

KASSANDRA.

To Troy already I foretold her woes. 1210

CHORUS.

How couldst thou pass unscathed of Loxias' ire?

KASSANDRA.

No man believed me—my sin's wage was this.

CHORUS.

Yet seem to us these thy soothsayings true.

KASSANDRA.

Ah me! ah me! Woe for the curse, the curse!
Again they rack me, prophecy's dread throes

With terror-prelude agonizing me!
See ye yon shapes upon the roof that sit—
Babes, like unto the phantoms of a dream?
Children, slain as it were by their own kin,
With hands filled full of their own flesh for meat, 1220
Grasping their hearts, their entrails, full in view,
Most piteous load, which their own father ate!
Vengeance for this, I tell thee, a craven lion,
Home-skulker from the wars, is plotting now
Against the hero on whose couch he lolls,
My lord—since needs must I bear thraldom's yoke.
Ah! the fleet's chieftain, who laid Troy in dust,
Knows not what treason yonder hell-hound's tongue
By fair speech long drawn out, an Atê lurking
Ambushed, shall bring to pass—a curse on her! 1230
This deed she dares—a woman slays her lord!
What loathly monster shall I name her now,
And err not?—'Snake two-headed?'—or a Scylla
Haunter of rock-clefts, bane of mariners?
Or raging dam of Hades, breathing out
For her lord truceless war?   She shouted o'er him,
All-reckless, as men shout for battle turned.
She feigns rejoicing for his safe return.
Heed me or not, 'tis all one: wherefore fret?
That which shall be will come. Right soon shalt thou
Pitying confess me all too true a seer.   [1240

CHORUS.

Thyestes' banquet on his children's flesh
Shuddering I recognise, and awed am I
To hear this o'er-true tale in nothing feigned.
The rest—wide of thy boding's track I run.

KASSANDRA.

Agamemnon's doom, I say, thou shalt behold.

CHORUS.

Peace, wretched maid! Hush thine ill tongue asleep!

KASSANDRA.

Ay, sooth, no Healer-god attends this word.

CHORUS.

No! if it come to pass—which God forbid!

KASSANDRA.

Thou dost but *pray*—at murder's work are these! 1250

CHORUS.

What man hath taken this foul deed in hand?

KASSANDRA.

Utterly hast thou missed my boding's drift.

CHORUS.

I grasp not its accomplisher's device.

KASSANDRA.

Yet all too well I know your Hellene tongue.

CHORUS.

So Pythian oracles do; yet dark are they.

KASSANDRA.

O me! what fire is this climbs o'er mine head!
Woe's me, Light-king Apollo, woe is me!
Yon human lioness that with the wolf
Coucheth, while stays afar the nobler lion,

Shall slay me, wretched me ! and with the cup   1260
Of vengeance shall she blend my punishment :
And vaunts, while for her lord she whets the brand,
Of death-wage waiting him who brings me hither.
Why then wear I these mockeries of myself—
The staff, the wreaths prophetic on my neck ?
These, ere mine own doom come, will I destroy.
Down to destruction ye !—I follow soon.
Make rich some other lost wretch in my stead !
Behold ! Apollo's self is stripping me
Of prophet-vesture !   Me he long hath watched   1270
In these arrayed, a very laughing-stock
Of kin unkind—all wrong with one accord !
They called me vagrant, juggling mountebank,
A starveling beggar-wretch : and I bore all.
And now the Seer hath unmade me, his seer,
And haled me captive to this doom of death.
For my sire's altar, waits the heading-block
For me, to reek hot with the victim's blood.
Yet not by Gods all outlawed shall I die :
For mine avenger shall hereafter come,   1280
The mother-slayer, his father's nemesis.
The wandering exile shall from banishment
Return, to set doom's topstone on his house.
For a great oath has by the Gods been sworn
That his dead father's corse shall draw him home.
What do I moaning pitifully here ?
Since I beheld erewhile our Ilium-town
Faring as she hath fared, and in such plight
By the Gods' sentence those her captors are,
I too will go, will brace myself to die.   1290
Lo, as the gates of Hades greet I these.
I pray to feel one mortal stroke—but one ;

That without anguish-throe, while ebbs my blood
In pangless death, so I may close mine eyes.

CHORUS.

O thou thrice-hapless woman and thrice-wise,
Long speech hath thine been!   Yet, if this thy doom
Truly thou knowest, why unfaltering pace
To the altar, like some consecrated steer?

KASSANDRA.

Escape is brought no nearer by delay.

CHORUS.

At least time's vantage hath the last to die.   1300

KASSANDRA.

Mine hour is come—small gain were won by flight.

CHORUS.

A resolute woman thou, a dauntless soul!

KASSANDRA.

Nay but 'tis something like a queen to die.

CHORUS.

Oh hapless who win such pathetic praise!

KASSANDRA.

Woe for thee, father, and thy noble sons!
  (Goes to the palace-door, and recoils from it.)

CHORUS.

What meaneth this?—what horror turns thee back?

KASSANDRA.

Pah!

CHORUS.

What sickens thee ?—is't aught thy soul abhors ?

KASSANDRA.

Murder : the house reeks all adrip with blood.

CHORUS.

How ?—this is scent of incense from the hearth. 1310

KASSANDRA.

It is a very charnel-house's breath !

CHORUS.

Thou dost misname the balm of Araby.

KASSANDRA.

I go—yea, therewithin to wail mine own
And Agamemnon's doom : enough of life.
Ah strangers !
Not at a bush, like bird once limed, I quake
For naught.   Bear ye this witness to my death,
When, for the woman me, a woman dies,
And, for a man mismated, falls a man.
I, on death's threshold, do but beg this boon.   1320

CHORUS.

Brave heart, I pity thy foreboded fate.

KASSANDRA.

Once more I fain would utter speech—no dirge
Over myself : I pray for this last time
The sun's light, that mine hateful murderers
May all at once to mine avengers pay
Quittance for this slain thrall, this helpless prey.

Ah, human life !—when most it prospereth,
'Tis but a pencil-outline.   Let fate frown—
Dashed with a wet sponge all the picture fades . . .
Sadder than mine I count the common lot.   1330
(Enters the palace.)

CHORUS.

Who hath drunken his fill of the chalice
    Of happiness ?   Who from the door
Ever thrust her of proudest palace,
    Crying, ' Enter thou here never more ! '
To our King have the Blessèd Ones given
    To lay waste Priam's town,
And he comes, by the Lords of Heaven
    Hither brought home with renown.
Yet now, if his blood must atone
    For some that were long since slain,
If his death for a slaughtered one
    Be a link in the vengeance-chain,   1340
Who among mortals shall dare,
    When he heareth his story, scorn
The lesson thereof, and declare
    ' 'Neath a happier star was I born ? '

AGAMEMNON *(within).*

O me !   I am stabbed deep with a mortal blow !

CHORUS I.

Hist !—Who crieth ' *I am stabbed* ? ' Who there is
    wounded mortally ?

AGAMEMNON *(within).*

O me !—they stab me yet the second time !

CHORUS 2.

Done already is the deed, meseems, by Agamemnon's
    cry !
Nay, in common counsel join we : safety shall be
    found thereby.

CHORUS 3.

For me, this is my counsel unto you :
Call the folk hither, raise the rescue-cry.

CHORUS 4.

Into the palace break forthright, say I,   1350
And by the dripping sword convict the deed.

CHORUS 5.

Such is my counsel : thus I cast my vote—
Be something done.   No time for dallying this !

CHORUS 6.

Nay, that is clear : they are in act to raise
Their usurpation's ensign o'er the town.

CHORUS 7.

We trifle time.   They trample underfoot
All semblance of delay.   Their hand sleeps not.

CHORUS 8.

I cannot tell what counsel should be best.
'Tis his to counsel who is ready to act.

CHORUS 9.

Yea, so think I ; for I discern no art   1360
Whereby with words to raise from death the dead.

Chorus 10.

How ?—basely cling to life, and crouch and cringe
To these usurping lords who shame the house ?

Chorus 11.

Nay, 'twere past bearing !   Better far to die.
Death were a milder doom than tyranny.

Chorus 12.

Shall we, from tokens darkly vague as cries
Of pain, divine that dead a warrior lies ?

Chorus 13.

We may not, ere we know, break into wrath.
Conjecture and clear knowledge are not one.

Chorus 14.

This rede, which all give, hath my full assent,   1370
Clearly to learn how Agamemnon fares.

*(The back-scene opens, displaying corpses of Agamem-
     non and Kassandra. Klytemnestra steps forward.)*

Klytemnestra.

Much in time past I spake to serve the time,
And blush not now to speak contrariwise.
Else, how should one who plots the doom of foes,
False friends, stake round them toils of mischief, raise
A net-wall higher than the prey may leap ?
This struggle—I planned it long since, brooding aye
On that old wrong.   O late my vengeance came !
Now all is done : firm stand I where I smote.
And so I wrought—O, I deny it not !—   1380
That he could flee not nor avert his fate.

A gapless net in fisher-wise I drew
Round him, a web with ample verge of doom.
I smote him—twice: two wild shrieks, and his limbs
Sank nerveless down; and, even as he lay,
A third I dealt, in thanks for answered prayer
To Hades, Saviour of the earth-veiled dead.
So, as he fell, he gasped his life away;
And spirting forth the sharp strong gush of gore
He dashed me with the dark spray, murder's dew, 1390
Who joyed as joys sown land to feel the boon
Of God's rain in the travail of the ear.
Since thus it is, O Argive elders, now
Rejoice, if ye can joy: I—I exult!
If one might make libation o'er a corpse,
Well might I over this, ay, more than well.
The bowl of all the accursèd ills he brimmed
In his own house, himself came home to drain.

CHORUS.

I marvel at thy tongue's bold hardihood,
Who mouthest out such vaunt above thy lord!   1400

KLYTEMNESTRA.

Ye look to cow me like some witless quean :
But I with heart unawed to you who know
Speak :—whether thou hast wit to praise or blame
Is all one :—this is Agamemnon, late
My lord, a corpse.   This hand that did the deed
Wrought righteousness.   The truth is as I say.

CHORUS.   *(Str.)*

Woman, what poison hast eaten, what drug that hath
      cursed earth's womb,

Drunk of what potion envenomed upcast with the
    sea's bitter spume,
  Thou o'er whose altar the sacrifice-smoke is the
    curse of a nation?
Traitress and murderess!—henceforth be thou cityless,
  Monster, the whole land's execration!   [1410

KLYTEMNESTRA.

On me thou passest sentence!—banishment
And hate of Argos, and a nation's curse—
Yet didst not move a finger against this man,
Who—heeding *her* fate no more than a beast's
Where sheep swarm countless in their fleecy herds,—
Slaughtered his child, of all my travail's fruit
Most dear, a charm to lull the Norland winds.
Him ought ye not have banished from the land
For his foul sin?   But, hearing of my deeds,   1420
A stern judge art thou!   Now I say to thee,
E'en threaten on—prepared am I to meet
All force with force—to lord it over me;
But vanquish first!   If God rule otherwise,
Thou shalt learn sanity—o'erlate for thee.

CHORUS.   *(Ant.)*

Haughty of spirit art thou, overweening the words of
    thy lips:
Raveth thy soul as one cursed by a fate wherein shed
    blood drips!
  Plain to behold on thy brow is the stain of murder's
    pollution
Still unavenged!   Thou shalt yet, of helpers forsaken,
    be met
  By the sword that shall deal thee the sword's
    retribution.   1430

KLYTEMNESTRA.

Now must thou hear this ordinance of mine oath—
By the accomplished vengeance for my child,
By Atê, Erinnys, unto whom I slew him,
Mine expectation treads no Hall of Fear,
So long as burns one flame upon mine hearth,
Ægisthus, loyal to me as heretofore :
For my stout shield of confidence is he.
Low lies yon man, his wife's dishonourer,
That fondling of Chryseïds many at Troy :
Low lies his captive thrall, the portent-seer   1440
Who shared one bed with him, the soothsayer
His couchmate leal, who on the ship-thwarts sat
Close-nestling to him.   These have their deserts !
He, even as I have said : she, like a swan,
Hath chanted her last strain, a dirge of death,
And lies, his darling, there.   She hath dressed for me
A dainty bridal-dish for my delight.

CHORUS.

Not with agony-throe
On my frame may he leap,
Nor with long-delayed blow
Round my sick-bed creep—
Yet oh, might Death come to me straightway, and
bring me the morningless sleep !   1450

For my guardian, my lord
Low, low hath been brought :
For a woman he warred,
And great deeds hath he wrought—
And behold, by a woman his life and the glory thereof
are made nought !

Oh madness of lust
  Of Helen, through whom
Were multitudes thrust
  Through the gates of the tomb !
One woman—and she before Troy unto lives without
  number was doom !

Unwashed, unforgot
  Lay the old murder-stain :
Thou hast made the dark blot
  Blush crimson again ;
And the ancient feud of the house is become its
  master's bane.   1460

KLYTEMNESTRA.

Tush, pray not for death
  As in grief for deeds past,
Neither Helen with breath
  Of a curse do thou blast
As the murderess, bane of her people, the woe that
  for ever shall last.

CHORUS.

Fiend, this work is thine
  Who dost swoop with foul wings
On the twin-branchèd line
  Of the Tantalid kings,
Thine this armèd rebellion of women, a horror my
  spirit that stings.   1470

As a raven stands tearing
  The corpse of one slain,

F

So stands she all-daring
  O'er him, and the strain
Of her triumph she chanteth, her exultation's jarring
  refrain.

KLYTEMNESTRA.

True word was that same
  When the Fiend thrice-great
Of this house thou didst name:
  For the blood-lust of hate
Evermore he rekindleth, and fresh wounds are dealt
  ere the old pang abate.   1480

CHORUS.

Of a fiend hast thou vaunted
  Who is strong to prevail,
Whose fury hath haunted
  This house for its bale—
Alas, the insatiate ruinous Fate of thine evil tale!

Ah, 'twas done as He willed
  Who is First Cause of all!
When is purpose fulfilled
  Of man, save as thrall
Of Zeus?—what thing of all these did not He fore-
  ordain to befall?

Oh my King! oh my chief!
  For thee how shall I cry?
How shall love wail its grief,   1490
  While thou so nigh
Foully slain in this web of a spider outgasping thy
  life dost lie?

Woe for yon bed!
  Tamely slain like a slave
There my King lieth dead,
  Thrust down to the grave
By the steel in the fingers of treachery clutched, by
  the two-edgèd glaive!

KLYTEMNESTRA.

And dar'st thou maintain
  That of me it was done? . . . .
By no wife was he slain,
  This Atreus' son;
But in shape of the wife of this corpse did the ancient
  terrible one,   1500

The Avenging Sprite,
  To exact the price
Of the foul feast dight
  By Atreus, arise,
And for babes once slaughtered he claimed this man
  for the sacrifice.

CHORUS.

Who shall witness for thee
  That thine hands are clean—
Ah, how can it be?—
  Of this murder, O Queen?
Yet—yet the ancestral Avenger may well thine
  accomplice have been;

For onward, unstayed
  As a torrent in flood,   1510

Dark Havoc doth wade
   Through kindred blood
Till he come to the day of atonement for babes that
   were slaughtered for food.

Oh my King! oh my chief!
   For thee how shall I cry?
How shall love wail its grief
   While thou so nigh
Foully slain in this web of a spider outgasping thy
   life dost lie?

Woe for yon bed!
   Tamely slain like a slave
There my king lieth dead,
   Thrust down to the grave
By the steel in the fingers of treachery clutched, by
   the two-edgèd glaive!   1520

KLYTEMNESTRA.

Treachery!—*mine?*
   His treachery first
Polluted his line
   With child-murder accurst
Of Iphigeneia, for whom fell my tears in a torrent-
   outburst!

Is this child-slayer's doom not
   The child-slayer's meed?
Ha, let him presume not
   In Hades to plead
Against me!—for the steel hath avenged her whom he
   by the steel made bleed.

CHORUS.

My mind is distraught :   1530
 Yea, hid from mine eyes
Be the pathways of thought ;
 And I cannot devise
Whither to turn in this hour when the house in ruin
lies.

 Lo, the blood-rain of doom !—
  The first droppings are o'er—
 It is sapping the home :
  My heart quakes at its roar !
Hark ! Fate on new whetstones is whetting the
vengeance of one wrong more !

 Oh Earth, that mine eyes
  Had been dark 'neath thy veil
 Ere I saw how he lies
  On this bed of bale   1540
'Twixt the silvern walls of the bath ! Who shall bury
him ?—who shall bewail ?

 Wilt thou dare such a thing—
  Even thou who didst slay !—
 With thy death-dirge to wing
  Thy lord's soul on its way ?
For his mighty achievements such graceless grace
wouldst unrighteously pay ?

 Ah, who shall upraise
  O'er the godlike dead
 The death-chant of praise ?
  What mourner shall shed
Tears, and with sorrow unfeignèd the path to his
grave-mound tread ?   1550

KLYTEMNESTRA.

Not unto thee
  Doth this care appertain :
By me, even me,
  Did he fall, was he slain :
I will bury him, I—but not with laments of his
  household-train ;

  But his daughter shall meet him,
    As fitting it is,
  With embraces shall greet him,
    And welcoming kiss :
By the swift-flowing River of Anguish shall Iphigeneia
  do this !

CHORUS.

The reproach that I said   1560
  Is hurled back in my face !
He were hardly bestead
  Who would judge in such case.
Lo, how the spoiler is spoiled, how the slayer atone-
  ment pays !

  Stands the ordinance sure
    While the years of Zeus run,
  That in suffering the doer
    Pay for all he hath done.
From this house who shall banish the curse-brood ?—
  with ruin 'tis knit into one.

KLYTEMNESTRA.

Now dost thou attain
  To true doctrine at last.

But for me, I were fain
To make oath-plight fast
With the fiend of the Pleisthenid house, to consent
unto all that is past,   1570

Be it never so grievous,
So he, through all days
Hereafter, would leave us,
To some strange race
Forth passing, with bloodshed of kin to afflict the
same in our place.

Lo, for me it were well
To have scant wealth-store,
So I might but dispel
That cloud evermore
Which hath darkened with madness of murder-re-
venges these halls from of yore.

Enter Ægisthus.

ÆGISTHUS.

Hail, gracious light of retribution's day !
Now I confess that the avenging Gods
On earth's abominations look from heaven,
When I behold this man, glad sight for me,   1580
Here lying in the net the Erinnyes wove
Punished for plots his father's hand contrived.
For Atreus, king of Argos, this man's sire,
Drove forth from home and city, a banished man,
My sire Thyestes—the plain truth is this—
His brother, rival with him for the throne.

Then suppliant to his hearth returning back,
Hapless Thyestes won reprieve from doom,
That his life-blood stained not his native soil:—
But Atreus, godless father of yon man,   1590
Feigning, with hate that smiled all eagerness,
A banquet-day to welcome home my sire,
Set on the board for meat his children's flesh.
The feet, the comb-like fingers of the hands,
In secret from the limbs he snapped away
That none might mark.   Unwittingly the sire
Ate food which was, thou seest, this house's doom.
Then, being made ware of that unholy deed,
Shrieked, reeled back from the butchery vomiting,
Cursed with an awful curse all Pelops' seed,   1600
Spurning the board in symbol of malison—
'*So perish all the line of Pleisthenes!*'
For this cause seest thou this man lying here;
And I am righteous plotter of his murder.
Me, yet a nursling, and my brethren twelve,
His father banished, with mine hapless sire:
Now, grown to man, hath Justice led me home,
And mine arm even from exile reached my foe;
For each device of this dark plot I framed.
Now would I hold it glorious to die,   1610
Who have seen this man in toils of Justice trapped.

CHORUS.

Ægisthus, insolence linked with guilt I scorn!
Thou say'st thou slewest this man wilfully,
The sole deviser of this piteous murder.
Thine head, be sure, in justice shall not 'scape
The curse of stoning at the people's hands.

ÆGISTHUS.

And this to me, from thee, at the lowest oar
Sitting—to me, throned on the upper tier !
Thou shalt learn, dotard,—learn a bitter lesson
For one so old—discretion's hest shalt learn !   1620
Bondage and hunger-pangs physicians are
Right skilful, even to school the stubbornness
Of old age.   Having eyes, canst see not this ?
Spurn not the goad, lest thou in misery fall.

CHORUS.

Woman !—didst thou, home-skulker, wait till men
Came home from war, shaming a hero's bed
The while, and plot a hero-chieftain's doom ?

ÆGISTHUS.

What, knave, these malapert words shall breed thee
    tears !
Far other tongue is thine than Orpheus had :
He drew all things by his song's witchery ;   1630
Thou, by thy witless yelpings angering us,
Shalt be thyself dragged, to be crushed and tamed.

CHORUS.

And thou forsooth shalt be the Argives' king—
Who, when thou hadst contrived this hero's death,
Dar'dst not with thine own hand do murder's work !

ÆGISTHUS.

By guile to take him was the wife's part, sure :
Me, as an ancient foe, suspicion watched.
But I by this man's treasure will essay

To rule this people.   Whoso disobeys
Shall, yoked in heavy bands, strain in the shafts, 1640
No full-fed trace-horse!   Hunger, pitiless
Dweller with darkness, shall behold him tame.

CHORUS.

Couldst thou not find it in thy dastard soul
To kill this man thyself, but his own wife,
Pollution of this land and of its Gods,
Must slay him ?   Ha, Orestes lives, I wot,
Lives to come hither home by fortune's grace,
And conqueror be and slayer of these twain !

ÆGISTHUS.

Since thou art determined so to do and speak, thou
    soon shalt know—
Up, my loyal comrades !   'Tis the hour for action !
    Guardsmen, ho !   1650

Guards of Ægisthus pour on to the stage.

CHORUS.

On then ye !—Let every man grip ready drawn the
    naked brand !

ÆGISTHUS.

Ay, and I shrink not from dying, so I perish sword in
    hand.

CHORUS.

Die—thou say'st ?   We hail the omen !   Victory for
    us, and life !

Enter Klytemnestra.

KLYTEMNESTRA.

Nay, my best-beloved; to evils past add not new
    curse of strife:
Surely in the deeds achieved a woeful harvest have
    we reaped:
Sorrow have we now enough; let hands no more in
    blood be steeped.
Pass thou—ancients, pass to homes that fate beneath
    our sway hath brought,
Ere ye do and suffer scathe.　These things must needs
    have so been wrought.
If the troubles past suffice you, we consent the past
    be past,
Whom the Avenger's heavy wrath hath smitten with
    misfortune's blast.　　　　　　　　　　　1660
Lo, a woman's rede is this, if any deign to learn
    thereby.

ÆGISTHUS.

But that these at me should flicker tongues that
    blossom vanity!—
Yea, should hurl against me railings such as these,
    and tempt their fate,
Wander wide from paths of prudence, and insult my
    kingly state!

CHORUS.

Ne'er shall this be Argives' wont, to cringe to villain
    reprobate!

ÆGISTHUS.

Ha! but I will surely visit this on thee in days to
    come!

CHORUS.

Nay, not thou!—if haply God shall guide Orestes
    hither home!

ÆGISTHUS.

Tush! I know the food of exiles—hope, a never-fruit-
    ing flower!

CHORUS.

Work thy pleasure : batten, fouling justice, while it is
    thine hour!

ÆGISTHUS.

Thou shalt yet, be sure, requite me for thy folly
    babbled now!   1670

CHORUS.

Vapour with a valorous mien, a cock beside his harem
    thou!

KLYTEMNESTRA.

Reck not thou of these, to heed their empty yelpings :
    thou and I,
Rulers now of town and palace-halls, will rule them
    royally.

                               [*Exeunt Omnes.*

CHOEPHOROE,

OR

THE MOURNERS.

ARGUMENT.

WHEN *the sin of Ægisthus and Klytemnestra began,
they sent away Agamemnon's young son, Orestes, to the
far land of Phocis, where King Strophius warded him
safely, and Pylades the king's son loved him as a
brother. So, when seven years, as Homer tells, had
passed since the murder of Agamemnon, and Orestes
was grown to man, he went to the oracle of Delphi,
and inquired of Apollo what he should do to avenge
his father, and to recover his inheritance; and the god
bade him slay the murderers, straitly commanding him
in no wise to spare his mother.*

*And herein is told how he returned secretly to
Mycenæ, and found there his sister Electra, who
dwelt in great affliction and abasement, by reason of
her love for the dead, and how these twain devised and
accomplished the bidding of the oracle.*

In translating this play I have generally adopted
the interpretation, and sometimes the reading, of Dr.
Tucker's edition of the 'Choëphoroe.'

DRAMATIS PERSONÆ.

ORESTES, *son of Agamemnon.*

PYLADES, *his friend, son of Strophius King of Phocis.*

ELECTRA, *daughter of Agamemnon.*

KLYTEMNESTRA, *wife and murderess of Agamemnon.*

ÆGISTHUS, *sharer in the guilt of Klytemnestra.*

NURSE.

DOOR-KEEPER.

MESSENGER.

CHORUS, *consisting of Trojan captives, handmaids of
the palace.*

SCENE :—In front of the Palace at Mycenæ.

CHOEPHOROE,
OR
THE MOURNERS.

Enter Orestes and Pylades.

ORESTES.

NETHERWORLD Hermes, steward of thy Sire's powers,
My saviour be and ally ; hear my prayer !
For to this land from exile back I come,
And on this grave-mound to my father cry
To hear my voice, to hearken my appeal.
This lock, my nurture's due to Inachus,
This too, my mourning-offering, I shear ;
For not by thee I stood to wail thy fate,
Father, nor waved thy grave-borne corpse farewell.

.   .   .   .

Ha ! what is this I see ?—what concourse draws   10
Hither of women in black vesture clad ?
What stroke of fate shall I divine herefrom ?
Hath some new trouble lighted on the house ?
Or guess I aright, divining that these bear
Balm to the dead, drink-offerings to my sire ?
Nought else may this be ; for methinks I see
My sister Electra pacing there in grief
Pre-eminent.   Grant me, Zeus, to avenge my sire !
Be of thy grace a champion unto me !

Pylades, stand we aside, that I may learn   2O
Surely what means this suppliant maiden-train.

                              [*Exeunt.*

Enter Electra, with Chorus, bearing libations.

Chorus.   *(Str. 1)*

Forth of the doors of the palace
  In procession of woe have I sped,
With drink-offerings brimming the chalice,
  With hands raining blows on mine head,
With cheeks scored with furrows red-staining
  The fingers that do them despite,
With a heart that hath tears of complaining
    For its meat day and night.

Lo, how for sorrows unending
  My raiment is utterly marred ;
Lo, how with comfortless rending
  The fair-woven vesture is scarred,
The vesture whose fold on my bosom
  Unseemly buffeted lies
Since calamity withered the blossom   30
    Of smiles from mine eyes.

(Ant. 1)

For a horror prophetic, heart-thrilling,
  Made the hair of our flesh uprise :
Out of slumber it shook us, filling
  Our ears with wrathful cries.
Out of hollows of darkness calling
  Came a voice at the midnight hour
Terror-winged, like a thunderbolt falling
    On the women's bower.

Then they unto whom divination
  Of vision and dream appertained
Spake by the Gods' inspiration
  As men by the truth constrained,
Spake, saying, ' A slain man, lying
  In the grave, for the vengeance due   40
In exceeding wrath is crying
    Against them who slew.'

                    (Str. 2)

And the godless woman is sending
  Me—O Earth Mother!—to pay
A graceless grace, that impending
  Ills may be turned away.
Yet to pour on the grave the oblation,
  And to utter the prayer, I dread:
O, how can there be expiation
    For the life-blood shed ?

Woe for the hearth polluted,
  The hearth that is misery all,
For the ancient stock disrooted,
  For the house that bows to its fall !   50
A sunless night hath enshrouded
  In darkness of all men abhorred
The house that is curse-overclouded
    Through the death of its lord.

                    (Ant. 2)

Invincible, quenchless, unfailing
  Loyalty spake of yore
In men's ears, wrought all-prevailing
  In their hearts—it is found no more:
Only the strong hand fear they;
  Yea, power, that holdeth the rod

O'er their heads, as a god revere they,
  Nay, more than a god.   60

Yet Justice is watching, to humble
  The haughty : her swift dooms smite
Some at midnoon ; some stumble
  On the marches of darkness and light
Ere the pangs long-evaded, that followed
  Aye, turn their bliss unto gall.
Some—have they escaped ?   They are swallowed
  In night that ends all !

(Str. 3)

When earth, man's nurse, hath once drunk in the
     life-blood's red pollution,
  The stain that cries for vengeance lies, a never-
     cleansèd clot ;
Even so the Curse that hoards for sin long pangs of
     retribution
May tarry while the all-cankering thing, his soul's
     disease, is ripening ;
       But ne'er forgetteth, spareth not. ·

(Ant. 3)

As remedy is none, nor cure, when once the portals,
     keeping   70
  Inviolate the maiden state, by outrage opened
     stand,
So all the multitudinous seas in one tide-race on-
     sweeping
Will roll their waters all in vain for cleansing, when
     foul murder's stain
       Hath once incarnadined the hand.

(Epode.)

And I—the Gods have crushed me in the fall
  Of my far-off war-leaguered home,
Have haled me from my fathers' house, a thrall,
    Unto an evil doom.
And I must brook the brutal recklessness—
  My life is not mine to control—
Which calls injustice justice, must suppress   80
    The loathing of my soul.
And I, to hide my tears, must veil mine head,
  Weeping the fate of my true chief,
A glory ruined ; and my heart seems dead,
    All frost-benumbed by grief.

Electra.

Ye handmaid-thralls, the palace-garnishers,
Since ye with me in this our suppliant-train
Are joined, be touching this my counsellors :—
When on his grave I shed these funeral bowls,
Offenceless how shall I invoke my sire ?
Shall I say, ' This from loving wife I bear
To her loved lord '—*my mother being that wife ?*   90
I dare not this : I know not what to say,
While on my father's grave this draught I pour.
Or shall I say this, after all men's wont—
' Oh grant thou fair return to those who send
These wreaths—*ay, some gift worthy of their crimes ? '*
Or in unhonoured silence, even as died
My father, shedding these for earth to drink,
Step back, as who casts out pollution, dash
The bowl to earth with unreverted eyes ?
O friends, be ye my counsellors herein ;   100
For in yon halls have we one common hate.

For dread of none hide aught your hearts within :
Fate's ordinance awaiteth both the free
And him that 'neath another's hand is thrall.
Speak, if thou hast aught better than my words.

CHORUS.

Revering as an altar thy sire's tomb
I will speak, for thou biddest, all mine heart.

ELECTRA.

Speak, as thou reverencest my father's grave.

CHORUS.

Pouring, speak solemn words for loyal souls.

ELECTRA.

And who be these whom of my friends I name ?   110

CHORUS.

Thyself first; whoso hates Aegisthus next.

ELECTRA.

For me and thee, then, thus shall I invoke ?

CHORUS.

This with thyself rests to discern and judge.

ELECTRA.

Whom then beside do I count for one with us ?

CHORUS.

Think on Orestes, though afar he be.

ELECTRA.

Well said : most meet thine admonition is.

CHORUS.

Then on that murder think; and for the guilty—

ELECTRA.

What shall I pray?   Instruct mine ignorance.

CHORUS.

That one—God—mortal—may against them come—

ELECTRA.

As judge or as avenger, wouldst thou say?   120

CHORUS.

Say plainly, ' One to render death for death.'

ELECTRA.

Nay, but were such prayer righteous in Heaven's
    sight?

CHORUS.

Not righteous !—to requite foul wrongs on foes?

ELECTRA.

(Going forward to the grave).
Great Herald of the Lords of Heaven and Hell,
Help, Hermes of the Shades!   O summon me,
To hear my prayers, the Gods of Underworld,
The awful Watchers o'er my father's house,
And earth herself, which brings all things to birth,
Which nurtures, and takes back their increase—thus !
(She pours from the bowl).
I, pouring these drink-offerings to the dead,
I, calling on my sire, cry, ' Pity me   130
And dear Orestes !   How shall we win home ?
For outcasts are we now ; we are chattels sold

By our own mother ; her price, a paramour !—
Aegisthus, who conspired to spill thy life !
I am but as a slave, and from his rights
Exiled Orestes lives ; they arrogantly
Are in the fruit of thy toils wantoning.
Oh, I implore thee, let Orestes come
Hither with fortune fair !   Hear, father, hear !
And to me grant a heart more virtuous far   140
Than is my mother's, and a hand more pure.
These prayers for us : but for our foes I pray
That thine avenger, father, may appear,
And that thy murderers righteously may die.
Thus I confront the sinners' wicked prayer :
I imprecate this curse upon their heads.
For *us*, O send these boons to the upper world !
So help Gods, Earth, and Justice victory-armed ! '
Thus pray I, pouring these drink-offerings.
Now rain ye flowers of lamentation down   150
Upon the dirge ye chant for him, the dead.

Chorus.

Shed ye your tears ! like the rain let them fall
  Spilt for the life of our lord which is spilt,
Shed on this grave-mound, the gateless wall
That shuts earth's evil and good from our lord,
  Shed to wash out the pollution of guilt
That were brought with his slayer's libation out-
    poured.
  Hear, O dread lord ! From the darkness that
    lies—
  Woe's me and alas !—on thy spirit's eyes
  Hear ! Let a strong spear-champion rise,   160
Rise to deliver thine house, whose hand

Shall strain the shaft on the Norland bow
With the strength of the War-god, shall close with
   the foe,
  And thrust to the hilt the brand!

ELECTRA.

      (Returning from the grave).
Now hath my sire the draught that earth hath
   drunk :—
But hear what strange tale from the grave I bring.

CHORUS.

Say on—mine heart for terror fluttereth.

ELECTRA.

This severed tress—I saw it on the grave!

CHORUS.

Hair of what man or what deep-girded maid?

ELECTRA. [170

A thing soon guessed : there's none but might divine.

CHORUS.

Old am I, yet from youth I fain would learn.

ELECTRA.

None living could have shorn such hair—save one.

CHORUS.

Nay, foes are they who should with shorn hair mourn.

ELECTRA.

This hair in gloss and hue is passing like—

CHORUS.

Unto what tresses ?   This I fain would learn.

ELECTRA.

To mine—to ours!—like sister-hair it shows.

CHORUS.

Ha !—can this be Orestes' secret gift ?

ELECTRA.

Exceeding like his curls doth it appear.

CHORUS.

Nay, hither how should he have dared to come ?

ELECTRA.

He shore, and sent, in homage to his sire.   180

CHORUS.

None the less weeping-ripe thy words make me,
If never more his foot may touch this land !

ELECTRA.

O'er me too sweeps heart-surge of bitterness :
I am stricken as by some deep-piercing shaft.
Burst from mine eyes, long drained of tears, the drops
Like thundercloud-outpourings after drought,
As I behold this tress !   How can I dream
That any Argive owned this lock, save one ?
'Twas never she, the murderess, shore it off,
My mother, she whose godless spirit of hate   190
To her own children, hath no touch of mother !
And I, oh could I but claim this outright,
This bright thing, for Orestes, best-beloved
Of men—ah, 'tis but hope that smiles on me !

Ah, that it had a messenger's glad voice!
Then, swayed no more 'twixt tide and tide of thought,
Then might I with sure knowledge spurn this tress,
As being severed from an enemy's head,
Or as my kindred might it mourn with me
Gracing this grave and honouring my sire.   200
Ah, but the Gods to whom I cry know all,
Know in what tempests, like men on the seas,
We toss.   If fate ordain that we escape,
From this small seed a noble stock may spring.
But lo, here footmarks be, a second sign!—
Yea, human footprints—like unto mine own—
Yea, here be twain, the outlines as of feet,—
His own and of his fellow-wayfarer!
The heels, the tendons' impress measured—thus—
With mine own footprints tally, line for line.   210
O travail-throes, O wilderment of soul!

Enter Orestes.

ORESTES.

Pray thou—first thanking Heaven for one prayer
Fulfilled—that all the rest may be vouchsafed.

ELECTRA.

Now what by Heaven's grace have I attained?

ORESTES.

Thou see'st him whom but now thou prayedst to see.

ELECTRA.

On whom call I, O thou who know'st mine heart?

ORESTES.

I know Orestes is thine heart's adored.

ELECTRA.

And what prayer answered, prithee, do I see?

ORESTES.

Lo, I am he : seek none more dear than me.

ELECTRA.

Stranger, wouldst weave a net of guile for me?   220

ORESTES.

Then were my plot devised against myself.

ELECTRA.

Nay, thou wouldst mock me in my misery!

ORESTES.

In mine own misery, if in thine, 'twere done.

ELECTRA.

Art thou Orestes?   Must I name thee thus?

ORESTES.

Thou seest my very self, yet doubtest me.
Thou sawest this lock, token of mourning love—
Thine heart's wings beat to think thou sawest me.
The print of mine own footsteps didst thou scan
Tokening thy brother's form matched with thine own.
Look on this lock, lay hair to severed hair :   230
And see this web, the work of thine own hand,
The shuttle-beats, the wild things there portrayed . .
Nay, curb thyself, be not for joy distraught :
I know our near kin are our bitter foes.

Chorus.

O dearest treasure of thy father's house,
Hope of a saviour-seed watered with tears !
Thy might shall win thee back thy father's home !

Electra.

Dear presence, dear with dues of fourfold ties
To me !   I may, I must, as father hail
Thee: and all love that round a mother clings 240
Is thine—most righteously is *she* abhorred—
And round that sister pitilessly slain !
My heart's one trust—O brother, glory mine,
Thou only ! . . Strength and Justice, with one more,
Zeus, of all mightiest, be on our side !

Orestes.

Zeus, Zeus, be thou beholder of our cause !
Look on that eagle-father's orphan brood—
Of him who died amidst the knots and coils
Of that fell viper.   Fatherless be these
And famine-wasted, being all too weak 250
Home to the nest to bring the father's prey.
So mayest thou behold us, me and her,
Electra, children of a sire bereft,
Both suffering one banishment from home.
If thou leave these to perish, brood of him
Who with high honour did thee sacrifice,
Whose hand like his shall pay thee banquet-dues ?
Lo, if thou leave thine eagle's brood to die,
Thou wilt have none to bear men tokens true,
Nor, if this royal stock should wither all, 260
Shall this thine altars serve on hecatomb-days.

Foster it, so to greatness shalt thou lift
From dust the house that now seems wholly fallen.

Chorus.

O children, saviours of your father's hearth,
Keep silence, younglings, lest one haply hear,
And for mere babbling's sake report all this
Unto our masters :—may I see them yet
Dead on the pyre mid spirting flame of pitch !

Orestes.

Me verily Loxias' mighty oracle
Will fail not : through this peril he bade press,   270
Cheering me on, and through my fevered heart
Breathing deep mutterings of a storm of doom,
If I pursued not my sire's murderers,
Bidding me, fierce as wild bull, slay the slayers
With vengeance by no blood-gild to be stayed—
Yea, said, except I did it, mine own soul
Should in fierce agonies atone for all.
For He—who shows men salves from earth that
    spring
For ills malign—these plagues He promised me :
Tetters that with fierce pangs crawl o'er the flesh, 280
Eating away its life and sap of youth,
While white hairs sprout all o'er the blasted skin ;
Yea, spake of onslaughts of the Avenging Fiends—
Ripe fruit whereof my father's blood was seed—
The shaft of darkness shot from the underworld
By suppliants murdered of their nearest kin ;
Madness, and phantom terrors of the night,
Which I, through darkness staring, plain should see,
Would harass, would torment their victim, till,

Torn by their brazen scourge, he is driven from
    men: 290
And such lost wretches neither in men's feasts
Have part, nor in the Gods' drink-offerings,
From altars by a father's unseen wrath
Banned: such none dare receive, none dwell with
    them.
They die at last the outcast's friendless death
By wasting doom to ghastly skeletons worn.
Shall I put no faith in such oracles?
Yea, though faith fail, yet must the deed be done:
For many promptings to one end conspire—
The God's behest, my great grief for my sire,   300
Yea, and the grim constraint of penury—
That I let not this people world-renowned,
Who overthrew Troy by their heroism,
Be thus two women's serfs—for womanlike
His heart is: if not, let him bide the test!

ORESTES *and* ELECTRA *take their stand on either
side of the tomb: the chorus group themselves round
it.*

THE INCANTATION CHANT.

CHORUS.

Destinies, Mighty Ones, grant that from Zeus may
    the issue betide
Even as Justice requireth, who now is arrayed on
    our side.
'Ever the tongue of hate shall the tongue of hate re-
    quite: 310
Aye for the stroke of murder the stroke of murder
    shall smite.'

Justice exacting her dues cries ringing-voiced this
    law.
' Doers must suffer '—so sayeth the immemorial saw.

ORESTES.   (Str. 1.)

What can I say, what do, O hapless father,
  So to waft down a light from 'neath our sky,
  Down to the narrow bed where thou dost lie,
Piercing the folds of gloom that round thee
    gather ?   320
Is it not so, that this our dirge, that singeth
Glories achieved, not all unwelcome ringeth
From these last Atreids, at thy doors who cry ?

CHORUS.   (Str. 2.)

My son, the spirit of the slain
  No ravening jaws of death-bale fire
Destroy : he flasheth forth again,
  Long after, lightnings of his ire.
Over the dead the keen is pealed ;
And lo, his murderer stands revealed.
When fathers foully butchered die,   330
The wail for justice, shrilling high,
Follows the track of wrong to exact the penalty.

ELECTRA.   (Ant. 1.)

Hearken, O father, then, as with strong crying
  We yet again weep forth the orphans' pain.
  Lo, on thy tomb we stand, thy children twain :
Heavenward ascends our lamentation's sighing.
Suppliants and exiles both thy grave hath found us !
Ah, is this well ?—are evils not all round us ?
  Wrestle we not with ruin all in vain ?

CHORUS. *(Str. 3)*

Yet out of all this God, so he be willing,   340
Shall waken shouts hereafter happy-thrilling;
  And, for the dirge that o'er the grave-mound rings,
  A triumph-chant shall hail in halls of kings
  The dear one who to us deliverance brings.

ORESTES. *(Str. 4)*

  But ah, that 'neath Ilium's walls,
    My sire, by a Lycian foe
    Spear-stabbed, thou hadst been laid low!
  Then renown hadst thou left in thine halls,
  And hadst made in the city's ways
  The life of thy children a praise;   350
    And a tomb in the land oversea
  Had a great host toiled to raise
    For their chieftain's memorial; and we
    Had been comforted for thee.

CHORUS. *(Ant. 2)*

How had the love there welcomed him
  Of old friends fallen gloriously!
Yea, in that nether kingdom dim
  He had towered august in majesty,
Approved a minister to stand
Before the Lords of Shadowland,
Who, while he lived, was overlord
O'er kings who accomplish fate's award   360
By sceptered sway of hearts, by battle-breaking sword.

ELECTRA. *(Ant. 4)*

  Yet I would not that thou, my sire,
    With other thy folk, unto whom
    The stroke of the spear dealt doom,

Before Ilium hadst lain on the pyre
Hard by Skamander's flow !
Nay, rather that even so
  By their own kin slain amid peace
Were those who have laid thee low,
  That far-away dwellers at ease   370
  Might hear of the doom of these.

     CHORUS.   *(Mesode.)*

Ah child, above earth's best fortune were this
 That thou namest : more precious were this than
  gold :
Not the dwellers in Fairyland know such bliss !
 Well mayst thou—the heart's wish lightly is told.
Yet oh, I hear it—the heavy sound
 Of the twin-lashed scourge of God draweth nigh !
Ay, the helpers of these lie 'neath the ground ;
But the hateful usurpers' hands are polluted
With blood : ere long shall their power be disrooted ;
 For now with the children is victory !

     ELECTRA.   *(Str. 5)*

Thy boding triumphant is in mine hearing 380
 Thrilling keen as the shaft that hath leapt from a
  bow !
 Zeus, Zeus sends up from the realms below
Retribution that long hath delayed its appearing
 To light on the felon hand all-daring—
 Yea, on that mother to fall unsparing !

     CHORUS.   *(Str. 6)*

O might it be mine, o'er the murderer foeman
 Murdered, to chant the triumph-song,

As he burns on the pine-logs, and over the woman,
  The traitress, to hymn the avengèd wrong!
For why should I hide how the vengeance-vision
  Aye hovers before me ? Mine heart's prow forward
  Driveth ; and bitter as blasts from norward   [390
Doth wrath's wind speed it on hate's stern mission.

ORESTES.   *(Ant. 5)*

Ah, when shall Zeus, in omnipotence baring
  His arm, reveal him the sinners' foe,
  Cleaving their heads with avenging blow ?
Then shall loyalty reign in a land well-faring.
  I cry for the righting of wrong: O hear me,
  Earth !—Underworld Powers, for mine help be near
    me !

CHORUS.   *(Ant. 3)*

A Law saith, ' Murder-drops of blood-libation   400
On earth spilt, cry for blood in expiation.'
  The Avenging Sprite shrieks, hastening Havoc on
  Which brings from graves of men dead long agone
  Ruin to crown the work of ruin done.

ELECTRA.   *(Str. 7)*

How long, how long ? Lords of the Shadow-regions,
  Look on us! Mighty Curses of the Dead,
  Look on us, banned our home and hard-bestead,
Last of the line that owned this land's allegiance!
  Whither may one turn, Zeus ?—is all hope fled ?

CHORUS.   *(Ant. 6)*

Thrilling and throbbing mine heart hath hearkened
  Unto thy wail: one while I despair,   [410
And I feel my spirit within me darkened
  As I list to thy passion of helpless prayer.

And anon cometh Hope, and she smileth in scorning
  Mine anguish away, bringing strength and uplifting
  Of soul, and the clouds from her face far-drifting
Reveal her, a glory, a splendour of morning.

ORESTES.   (*Ant. 7.*)

What shall we say, and err not ?   Dare we smother
    Flames of our anguished wrath for that blood-
      feast
    Lapped by our dam ?—O nay, 'twill ne'er be
      eased.   420
  Ay, and our heritage from that fierce mother
    Is the wolf-spirit whose hate is not appeased.

CHORUS.   (*Str. 8*).

I have lifted my voice in the Aryan keen, as a Kissian
      wailing
I shrill my lament, and mine arms may ye mark
      tossed to and fro,
As my hard-clenched hands from above are in swift
      succession hailing
On mine all-wretched head, till it rings with their
      buffetings, blow upon blow.

ELECTRA.   (*Str. 9.*)

Mother all-reckless in hate, thou didst cause like a foe
      to be borne   430
Unto burial a king unattended, a husband whom none
      would mourn,
Whom all unlamented thou daredst to thrust 'neath
      the earth as in scorn !

ORESTES. *(Str. 10.)*

Thou tellest our utterest shame, woe's me!—yet the
  shameful despite,
If the Gods will but help, if mine hands may avail,
  will I surely requite!
Then I care not though I die, having thrust her from
  life and from light.

CHORUS. *(Ant. 10.)*

Hacked limb from limb was his corse, know thou!—
  as she dealt with the slain, 440
So did she deal with his son, that thy life should be
  one long pain
Of exile. The pangs and the shame of thy sire—is
  their tale not plain?

ELECTRA. *(Ant. 8.)*

Thou tellest the fate of my sire:—me far from him
  then were they keeping
Flouted and scorned: like some pestilent hound was
  I kennelled apart.
Think ye I laughed as I poured out the tear-drops,
  with floods of weeping
Wailing in secret?—O hear it and grave it upon
  thine heart! 450

CHORUS. *(Ant. 9.)*

Draw it in deep through thine ears with the silent
  footfall of thought.
Such was the past: for the future let thy resolve
  burn hot:
Thou must enter the lists with a spirit to temper of
  steel fire-wrought.

ORESTES. (Str. 11.)

Father, I cry on thee; now be the ally of them that
    love thee!

ELECTRA.

Yea, and I lift up my voice, while the flood of my
    weeping flows.

CHORUS.

We shriek, as partakers with these, our invocation
    above thee.
Come to the light, and give ear: be our ally against
    our foes!   460

ORESTES. (Ant. 11.)

Let our might come to grips with their might, our
    right of their right make assaying!

ELECTRA.

Accomplish, ye Gods, our desire, as Justice pro-
    nounceth her doom!

CHORUS.

Trembling on me layeth hold, as I hearken the spell
    of your praying!
Long retribution hath tarried, but now at our prayers
    let it come!

    O dread death-grapple wherein these kindred close!
    O tuneless music of ruin's blood-stained blows!
    O lamentable pangs past all enduring!
    O anguish of the wound that baffles curing!   470
Yet of these shall the wound of the house find
    staunching now,

Yea, and from none of a stranger line, I trow:
These, these shall pace the grim feud's path blood-
    haunted.
Lo, to the Nether Gods this hymn is chanted.

Hear, Blessed Ones, deep under earth though ye be,
This our appeal, and your help send ye
Of your grace to the children, for victory!

ORESTES.

Father, who diedst in unkingly wise,
Grant to my prayer the lordship of thine halls!   480

ELECTRA.

Father, I too beseech thee—lo, I am sold
To Aegisthus: let me 'scape that deep reproach!

ORESTES.

So shall for thee the feast of use and wont
Be stablished: else, where feast the dead Kings, thou
Wilt sit shamed, banned from earth's burnt-offerings'
    steam!

ELECTRA.

From these old halls, of my rich heritage
Bridal libations will I bring to thee,
Yea, above all else honour this thy tomb.

ORESTES.

Earth, send my sire to captain me in fight!

ELECTRA.

Persephonê, crown him with fair victory!   490

ORESTES.

Think, O my father, on the bath of death!

ELECTRA.

Think on that strange net which they cast o'er thee!

ORESTES.

In gyves not brazen, father, wast thou trapped,—

ELECTRA.

But foully snared in palls of treachery.

ORESTES.

Father, shall these reproaches rouse thee not?

ELECTRA.

Wilt not upraise for love of us thine head?

ORESTES.

Send Justice, in fair fight to champion us,
Or let us trap them, as they thee, by guile,
If thou, once vanquished, wouldst in turn o'ercome.

ELECTRA.

And hear this, father, this our last appeal :   500
As on thy tomb thou seest thy nestlings crouched,
Compassionate thy daughter and thy son.

ORESTES.

And blot not out in these all Pelops' seed;
For thus thou art not dead, though thou have died.

ELECTRA.

For children keep alive a man's renown,
Though he be dead, as floats bear up the net,
Up-buoying from the abyss the flaxen line.

ORESTES.

Hearken ; for thy sake ring these wailings down :
Thyself art saved by granting this our prayer.

CHORUS.

Full measure hath this prayer ye have lengthened
    out   510
To grace the tomb, the fate unwailed before.
The rest now, since thy soul is thus resolved,
Straight do, and put thy fortune to the proof.

ORESTES.

That will I : yet 'tis pertinent to ask
Why sent she the libation, for what cause
Rues she too late a mischief nought may cure ?
To an undiscerning dead man was it sent,
This sorry boon ?—I cannot deem it so.
Yea, the gift falls so far short of the offence !
' Though one pour out his all for one man's blood 520
To atone, it is lost labour,' saith the saw.
Tell, if thou knowest, this : I fain would learn.

CHORUS.

I know it, son, for I was there.   By dreams
And haunting terrors of the night appalled
That godless woman sent these offerings.

ORESTES.

Heard ye her dream, to tell it certainly ?

CHORUS.

She dreamed she bare a serpent, herself saith.

ORESTES.

And the tale's end and consummation—what ?

CHORUS.

In swaddling bands she lulled it, like a babe.

ORESTES.

And what food did the new-born monster crave ? 530

CHORUS.

Herself gave to it in her dream the breast.

ORESTES.

Did it not wound her dug, the loathly thing ?

CHORUS.

Yea, with the milk it sucked forth clots of blood.

ORESTES.

Ha ! not for nought !—a vision of a man !

CHORUS.

Scared, from her sleep she sprang with one wild
    shriek :
Then for our mistress' help leapt into light
Lamps many through the halls, erst darkness-
    quenched.
So sends she these sepulchral offerings,
As who hoped these should charm away her doom.

ORESTES.

I pray this earth, I pray my father's tomb,   540
That this her dream may be in me fulfilled.
Right well, I judge, doth it agree thereto :
For if the serpent from the self-same womb
Proceeding, in my swaddling bands was swathed,
And mouthed the self-same breast that nurtured me,
And mingled with a clot of blood the milk,

And she for dread thereof in anguish shrieked,
She surely must, who nursed that portent dread,
By violence die ; and I, her serpent I,
Shall slay her, even as this dream foreshows.   550

CHORUS.

Herein I choose thee for my soothsayer.
So be it !   For what follows, tell thy friends
Both what to do and what to leave undone.

ORESTES.

'Tis soon said.   Let my sister pass within :
And I beseech you that ye hide my plot,
That they who slew a prince by treachery
By treachery may in this our net be snared,
And so die even as Loxias foretold,
Phœbus the King, true prophet from of old.
In stranger's guise I, garbed at all points so,   560
Will to yon outer gate with this man come,
Pylades, guest and ally of our house.
And we will utter both Parnassian speech,
Feigning the accent of the Phocian tongue.
And if no porter with blithe welcoming
Receive us—since curse-haunted is the house—
There will we tarry till the folk, that pass
The halls, thereat shall marvel, and shall say :
' Why thrusts he back the suppliant from his doors,
If in the land Ægisthus is, and knows ? '   570
And I, if once I pass the threshold-stone,
And find him throned upon my father's seat—
Or if he come and look me in the face,
Yea, cast his eyes upon me, be thou sure,
Ere he can say, ' Whence comes the stranger ? ' dead

I'll lay him, plunging through him the swift sword.
The Erinnys then, in slaughter stinted not,
Shall quaff her third draught—undiluted blood !
Now therefore, sister, watch well all within,
That this may fall with our aims consonant.　　580
And you I bid to bear a silent tongue :
Keep peace where needeth, and in season speak.
In all else, Hermes, be thou nigh to aid,
Speeding aright each venture of my sword.

> [*Exeunt Orestes, Pylades, and Electra.*

CHORUS.　　*(Str. 1)*

Many a horror, fell and dread,
Great All-mother Earth hath bred ;
'Twixt the deep sea's mighty arms
Man-destroying monster-swarms ;
Sudden torches flashed on high,
Flowers amid dark fields of sky ;　　590
Fearsome winged and fourfoot things,
And the tempest's fury-wings.

(Ant. 1)

But the spirit fierce and fell
Maddening man, ah, who can tell?—
Maddening women reckless-souled—
Tell the passion uncontrolled
Aye with human ruin joined—
Loveless lust of female kind
That doth wedlock's tree disroot　　600
In the man as in the brute ?

(Str. 2)

Let him ponder, whose wit not aimless,
　　As a bird wide-wandering, flies,
What purpose did cruel-shameless
　　Thestius' daughter devise—

A purpose of fire, for the casting
  Down on the red hearth-flame
Of the brand foredoomed twin-lasting
  With her son's life, even as he came
Forth of the womb sudden-crying ;   610
  For, while yet it abode unconsumed,
He should see not the day of dying
    Unto all men foredoomed.

(Ant. 2)

A hate shall she too be in story,
  Even Scylla of blood-stained hand
Who destroyed the Cretans' glory
  For love of the foe of her land.
For the necklace of gold she lusted,
  The gift that Minos bore,
And the lock wherein Nisus trusted,
  The tress immortal, she shore
From his head—O shameless-hearted !—
  As he breathed mistrustless of doom   620
In sleep—his soul waked, and upstarted,
    For Hermes said, ' Come ! '

(Str. 3)

Ah no, but these agonies olden
  Of sin may in no wise compare
With the curse in yon halls enfolden,
  With the union of horror there.
O adulterous, treacherous woman
  Who plotted the death of her lord,
The champion dreaded of foemen
  For the ruining wrath of his sword !
Ah, the hearth where runs not riot
  The flame of passion, the grace

Of a spirit meek and quiet
    In woman, I praise.   630

(Ant. 3)

Nay, of crimes 'tis the Lesbian beareth
  The palm ; ever loathèd it is
And bewailed : still one compareth
  Each ghastliest horror with this.
That race that with sin's defiling
  Was tainted, hated and banned
Of the Gods, a scorn and reviling
  Long since perished out of the land.
None honoureth, none relenteth
  Unto that which the high Gods curse.
I compare them—yea, Justice consenteth—
    Their sin and hers.

(Str. 4)

But the keen-whetted sword maketh severance
  Of the breath-ways of life, deep thrust   640
    By Justice's hand ; for the Right
    Transgressed is not spurned out of sight
    By them that would do despite
Unto Zeus, to deny him reverence
  Overstepping the path of the just.

(Ant. 4)

Lo, the anvil of Justice is planted
  Firm, and the swordsmith Fate
    Is forging the Sword of Doom :
    The deep-brooding Erinnys brings home
    The child Retribution, of whom   650
Shall the blood-pollution, that haunted
  The house, be avenged thus late.

The scene changes to the front of the palace.

ORESTES.

Ho! gate-ward, list my knocking at the door!
Who is within?—ho, gate-ward, once again!
Lo, the third time I cry, 'Come forth the house!'—
If great Aegisthus is the stranger's friend.

DOOR-KEEPER.

Ho there! I hear! Of what land art thou?—
whence?

ORESTES.

Bear word unto the masters of the house;
For 'tis to these I come, and tidings bring—
Nay, haste thee, for the dusky car of night   660
Speeds on, and time it is that wayfarers
Drop anchor in hospitable hostelry.
Let one who hath authority come forth—
The mistress—nay, her lord were seemlier;
For then for shamefastness words falter not
In mid-speech : man with confidence may speak
To man, and show clear tokens for his tale.

Enter Klytemnestra.

KLYTEMNESTRA.

Strangers, say whatso needeth.   Here have we
All that beseemeth such a house as this—
Warm baths, beds, all that charms away the pain 670
Of toil, observance of all courtesy.
If aught of weightier import needs to do,
This were for men, with whom we will confer.

ORESTES.

A Daulian stranger I, from Phocis come.
As, bearing mine own needments, on I fared
To Argos—whither now my feet have won—
A man I knew not met me who knew not him,
And asked my way, and told his own, and named him
Strophius the Phocian, in our conference, saying:
'Since thou to Argos goest in any wise,   680
Say to his parents—mark with diligent heed—
This—" Dead Orestes is : " forget it not.
If then it please his friends to bring him home,
Or in a strange land, exiled evermore,[1]
To bury, bring back word as they command ;
For now in brazen sides the funeral urn
Hideth his dust, his dues of mourning paid.'
So heard I, so I tell : if now I speak
Unto his house's heads and to his kin,
I know not ; but it fits his sire should know.[2] 690

KLYTEMNESTRA.

Ah me ! thy tale our utter ruin tells !
Curse of this house, O wrestler none may quell,
Aimer at prey from thy range well withdrawn,
Archer whose bow unerring slays from far,
Thou stripp'st me bare of dear ones—hapless me !
And now Orestes—ah, so wisely, he deemed,
He kept his foot clear of destruction's slough !—
Him, Hope the Healer, born to purge these halls
Of the Fiends' Revel, him thou writ'st down—thus !

1. Another interpretation : 'evermore our guest.'

2. To the speaker, in his assumed character, Orestes is a
mere name. He does not know his family history, and takes
for granted that his father is alive.

ORESTES.

n sooth, fain had I to such princely hosts   700
.s bearer of glad tidings made me known,
.nd my guest-welcome so had earned : for what
; kindlier than the tie of guest and host ?
'et to my thought it seemed an impious deed
'o do not this sad service to his friends
Vhen I had promised, and was greeted guest.

KLYTEMNESTRA.

one the less worthy thee shall be thy welcome,
or less the house shall hold thee for its friend.
nother had brought the tidings, hadst thou not.
ut now 'tis time that guests who all day long   710
ave journeyed far, be graced with service meet.
To *steward).*   Lead him to our guest-chambers
    dight for men,
7ith these his thralls and fellow-wayfarers ;
here be their tendance as beseems our house.
his do, as who shall give account to me.
ut I will tell this to the house's lord ;
nd—for we are not all bereft of friends—
7e will take counsel touching this mischance.

[Exeunt.

CHORUS.

7hen, O ye handmaids leal to the house, shall we lift
    up on high   720
trength of our voices, to shout for Orestes the good-
    speed cry ?
lighty Ones, Earth, and thou Grave-mound which
    over the body art laid

I

Of a king, of a captain of ships, now hearken, now
    come to our aid !
Now is it time, full time is it now, that with us be
    allied
Suasion of Guile, and that Underworld Hermes of
    Darkness be guide
To him who shall enter the strife which the slaughter·
    ing sword shall decide.

Enter Nurse.

Meseems the stranger bringeth grief with him :   730
Lo, yonder weeping comes Orestes' nurse.
Whither away, Kilissa, through the gates ?
No hireling sorrow fareth forth with thee.

NURSE.

Our lady biddeth summon with all speed
Ægisthus to her guests, that plainlier,
As man from man, he may enquire of them
Touching these tidings. From her household-thralls
Brows lowering veiled the laughter in her eyes,
Hiding her joy for what hath happed so well
For her, but for this house all-wretchedly,   740
By this the strangers' tale—alas, too plain !
Ah, glad at heart shall he be, hearing this,
Soon as he learns the story. Woe is me !
How all the mingled troubles of the past,
So hard to bear, that here in Atreus' halls
Befell, wrung in my breast this heart of mine !
But never pang like this have I endured.
All ills beside with patience still I bore :
But dear Orestes, love-load on my heart,

Whom from his mother I received and nursed— 750
Oft his shrill nightly summons broke my sleep:
Ay, many a fruitless hardship I endured:
For the unreasoning babe, like some young beast,
Sooth, must ye rear with mother-wit for guide;
For no speech hath the child in swaddling-clothes
To tell of hunger, thirst, or nature's need;
And straight the young frame heeds the imperious
    call.
Forewarned hereof, yet oft-times caught, I wot,
Unwares, 'twas mine to cleanse his swathing-bands;
So had the nurse the fuller's office too. 760
Such twofold handicraft I took on me
When I received Orestes for his sire.
And now I hear—woe's me!—that he is dead.
And to the man I go, who hath defiled
This house, and who shall hear this tale with joy!

CHORUS.

How furnished, prithee, doth she bid him come?

NURSE.

How?—say it again, that I may understand.

CHORUS.

To come with guards encompassed, or alone?

NURSE.

She bids him bring his spearman-retinue.

CHORUS.

Bear no such message to our hated lord! 770
Bid him alone come, and mistrustless hear,

Yea, come with all speed with a joyful mind.
' Crooked is set straight in the messenger's heart.'[1]

NURSE.

How now ?—Art thou for these their tidings glad ?

CHORUS.

What if Zeus turn to triumph this disaster ?

NURSE.

How should he—and our hope Orestes dead ?

CHORUS.

Not yet—this might the sorriest seer divine.[2]

NURSE.

What say'st thou ? Know'st thou more than meets the
    ear ?

CHORUS.

Go, bear thy message.   That enjoined thee, do.
The Gods take care for that for which they care. 780

NURSE.

Nay then, I go, and will obey thy words ;
And by the Gods' grace may all good betide.

[Exit.

CHORUS.   *(Str.* 1*)*

Now in prayer to thee I call, Zeus Father, Lord of all

1.   Understanding the line as a quotation of a bit of popular
casuistry in favour of mental reservation.

2.   Tucker interprets: ' As yet, 'twere no mean seer would
vouch for this.'   With this view accords the explanatory note of
the scholiast—' He were an unerring seer who could assert this.'

The Gods Olympian, prosper us, who yearn to see
the Right
In triumph stand assured o'er the wrong so long
endured.
All my cry is but for justice, Zeus: protect him
with thy might!

(Str. 2)

Ah, do thou, Zeus, of thy grace, but bring him face
to face
With his foes in yonder palace, in iniquity's strong-
hold;   790
For, if thou exalt him high, he shall render joyfully
Requital of thank-offerings twice and three times
over told.

(Ant. 1)

Think on him thou heldest dear: ah, behold his scion
here
To a chariot yoked of peril:—O set his course a
goal!
Oh to see his rushing feet keeping time and measure
meet,
Straining down the course to victory, upheld by thy
control!

(Str. 3)

Hearth-gods, who have your shrine where the house's
treasures shine,   800
Hear, all-propitious, hear! Exact atonement for
the blood
Of men murdered long agone! Lo, the murder old is
grown;
No more within yon palace may it spawn a cursèd
brood!

(Mesode.)

O Dweller in dark halls 'twixt thy chasm's massy
        walls,[1]

  Vouchsafe the hero's house may now uplift its head
        once more,   [810

May look with loyal eyes bright in the new sunrise
  From out the veil of darkness that hath hung its
        face before.

(Ant. 3)

Oh be Maia's Son allied, as right is, on our side,
  Who can speed an emprise onward like a ship
        before the wind,

He who prompts the word that throws darkness o'er
        the eyes of foes,
  Till they stumble in the daylight whom his craft
        has stricken blind.

(Str. 4)

Then at last will we upraise for deliverance songs of
        praise,   820
  And will banish all the wailing of the trembling
        chords of fear.

O then shall all be well; and my gain, ah, who shall
        tell
  When the curse is done away from them my heart
        holds dear ?

(Ant. 2)

O be stout of heart, my son, when the deed is to be
        done !

  She will shriek to thee, ' My child ! ' so to paralyse
        thine hand :

---

1. Apollo, in his Delphian shrine in the rifted rock of
Parnassus.

Then shout thy father's name o'er the deed his blood
    doth claim :
Then consummate the ruin wherein blameless thou
    dost stand.   830

                    (Ant. 4)
Thine be Perseus' heart, whose sword with monster-
    women warred,
When thou wreakest bitter vengeance for thy loved
    ones underground,
And for them on earth, to slake Ruin's blood-thirst
    for their sake,
And when the doom-deviser hath in thee destruction
    found.

Enter Ægisthus.

ÆGISTHUS.

Summoned by messenger express I come.
I hear how certain strangers hitherward
Faring, have brought us tidings nowise glad,   840
Orestes' death.   To charge the house therewith
Were laying a terror-raining murder-load
On one yet gashed and festering with old wounds.
How shall I know that this is truth unfeigned ?
Is it but women's panic-struck report
That leaps like flame, and dies down leaving nought ?
What can ye tell, that I be certified ?

CHORUS.

We have heard—but pass thou in, and of thy guests
Make question.   Nothing-worth are hearsay-tales
When man may question of a man himself.   850

ÆGISTHUS.

Myself will see and sift the messenger,
Whether himself was there, and saw his death,
Or speaketh but from some vague rumour heard.
My mind's keen vision shall he not delude.

[*Exit.*

CHORUS.

O Zeus, O Zeus, what shall I say, and where
Make a beginning with the vow and prayer ?
How shall my words, with utmost loyal intent,
Rise to the height of this great argument ?
Now are the keen blades, sped on murderous mission,
Bloodstained, at point to try the grim decision— 860
Perish shall Agamemnon's house, descending
Down into ruin utter and unending ?
Or shall Orestes kindle a beacon-light
For freedom and the lawful rule of Right,
And hold his father's wealth of empery ?
  O mighty strife wherein with these two foes
  He, sole avenger of the slain, shall close
In wrestle of death—for victory may it be !

ÆGISTHUS. *(within)*

Ah-h ! woe is me !

CHORUS.

  Ha !—hist !—the cry of one ! 870
How goes it ?—what in yon halls now is done ?
Stand we aloof while this deed is achieved,
That men may hold us guiltless of these ills ;
For the fight's issue is decided now.

Enter Servant.

SERVANT.

Alas and well-a-day for my dead lord !
Woe and alas ! and thrice-alas I cry !
Ægisthus is no more ! Fling wide the gates
With all speed, and unbar the doors that keep
The women's bowers !—There want young sinews
    here—
Not to defend him who is sped—what help ?   880
Ho there !—I hail the deaf, and vainly cry
To sleepers ! Whither is Klytemnestra gone ?
What doth she ?—Now is her neck like to fall—
'Neath Justice' sword—the edge hangs imminent !

Enter Klytemnestra.

KLYTEMNESTRA.

What now ? What clamour wak'st thou in the halls ?

MESSENGER.

The dead are slaying the living !—*this* I say.

KLYTEMNESTRA.

Ah me ! I understand thy riddling speech !
By guile we perish, even as we slew !
Give me—quick, give a warrior-quelling axe :
Let see if now I shall prevail or fall ;   890
For to this desperate issue am I come.

Enter Orestes.

ORESTES.

Thee too I seek : for him, it is enough.

KLYTEMNESTRA.

Ah me !—thou art dead, Ægisthus best-beloved !

ORESTES.

Lov'st thou the man ?—thou in one grave with him
Shalt lie.   In death shalt thou forsake him never.

KLYTEMNESTRA.

Forbear, my son !   Revere this, O my child,
This breast, whereon thou oft hast slumbered, whence
Thy lips the while drew life-sustaining milk.

ORESTES.

Pylades, must my reverence spare my mother ?

PYLADES.

Where then were Loxias' sun-clear oracles   900
Uttered at Pytho, and thy plighted oaths ?
Rather have all the world thy foes than Heaven.

ORESTES.

I adjudge thee victor : thou exhortest well.
Come : by his very side will I slay thee.
Living, thou held'st him dearer than my sire :
Sleep with him in thy death, since thou dost love
This man, and hatest whom thou ought'st to love.

KLYTEMNESTRA.

I nursed thee—O let me grow old with thee !

ORESTES.

My father's murderess !—shalt thou dwell with me?

KLYTEMNESTRA.

Fate was accomplice in those deeds, my child.   910

ORESTES.

Yea, Fate the while for thee prepared this doom.

KLYTEMNESTRA.

Nought dost thou dread a mother's curse, O child?

ORESTES.

My mother cast me forth to misery.

KLYTEMNESTRA.

Nay, to a home of friends she sped thee forth.

ORESTES.

Twice sold was I, a freeborn father's son!

KLYTEMNESTRA.

Sold?—and what price did I receive for thee?

ORESTES.

I shame to utter its reproach to thee!

KLYTEMNESTRA.

Thy father's sins—spare not to tell them, too!

ORESTES.

Sitter at home, accuse not him who toils!

KLYTEMNESTRA.

Hard is the lot of wives deserted, child.   920

ORESTES.

They sit at home, and by their lord's toil live.

KLYTEMNESTRA.

Thou seemest set to slay, O son, thy mother!

ORESTES.

Thou wilt be slayer of thyself, not I.

KLYTEMNESTRA.

See to it—'ware the mother's Vengeance-hounds!

ORESTES.

How should I 'scape my father's, if I spared ?

KLYTEMNESTRA.

Living, I wail as to a tomb—in vain !

ORESTES.

My father's fate wafts unto thee this doom.

KLYTEMNESTRA.

Woe's me, who bore this serpent and who nursed !

ORESTES.

Prophet indeed was that thy dream-born fear—
Unnatural murderess, die the unnatural death !   930
   [*Exit, dragging Klytemnestra within.*

CHORUS.

O but I wail the misery of these twain !
Yet, since to blood-guilt's topmost peak hath climbed
Hapless Orestes, rather this I choose
Than that the house's hope in ruin fell.

       (Str. 1)

On the children of Priam came heavy-handed
 Justice, exacting the penalty-pain ;
So to Agamemnon's halls came the banded
 Leash of lions, the war-gods twain ;[1]

1. Orestes and Pylades.

And the exile who followed the Pythian vision,   [940
Whom a God sped forth on his vengeance-mission—
  He hath come to his own : all, all doth he gain !

(Str. 2)

Raise gladsome acclaim for the house of our masters
Escaped from the curse, from the spoiling of wasters,
  Escaped from the path of an evil fate
  Whereon the defilers dragged it so late !

(Ant. 1)

Down swoopeth the guileful Retribution
  On the caitiff who shrinks from open fight ;
But her champion's hand mid the strife's confusion
  She grasped—Zeus' Daughter, whom Justice and
      Right
We mortals name who fitly before her   950
Bend, with acceptable prayers to adore her—
  And the breath of her wrath did the foe's strength
      blight.

(Str. 3)

So hath Loxias, Lord of Parnassus, striven,
  From where on its crest is his mighty shrine,
With her unto whom long respite was given,
  Who at last is enmeshed in the net divine.
  O yea, on the Gods by their nature is laid
  A constraint, that the wicked they may not aid.
It is meet to adore the Lords of Heaven,   960
  For at last upon us doth the dayspring shine.

(Ant. 2)

The curb from the lips of the thrall is taken !
Lift up thine head, house long forsaken
  Of freedom ! Long, O long didst thou bend
  Crushed to the earth as it seemed without end.

(Ant. 3)

Time, all-fulfiller, in swift revolution
  Shall come to the house, when far off flies
From the hearth of it banished all the pollution
  By curse-dispelling sacrifice;
  And fair-faced fortunes and gracious-eyed
  To the alien sojourners there shall betide   970
Once more, after all that long confusion :
  Yea, at last upon us doth the dayspring rise !

*The scene opens, and Orestes is seen standing beside
the bodies of Ægisthus and Klytemnestra.*

ORESTES.

Behold ye these two tyrants of the land,
My father's slayers who made his home a ruin.
Worship had they, once sitting on the throne :
They are lovers yet, as shows the fate they share,
And their oath-plight abides unbroken yet.
They plighted oath to slay mine hapless sire,
And be in death one—and the oath is kept.
Mark yet again, O hearers of these woes,   980

*(holds up the robe in which Agamemnon was entangled
at his murder)*

This death-gin, snare that trapped my hapless sire,
Gyves for his hands, linked shackles for his feet !
Unfold it wide, and in a ring stand round
To show a king's shroud, that the Sire may see—
Not mine, but He that on all this looks down,
The Sun-god—see my mother's foul, foul deeds,
That he may stand my witness at the bar
That on my mother righteously I wreaked
This doom—I speak not of Ægisthus' doom :

He hath the adulterer's lawful punishment—   990
Who for her lord devised this hateful thing,
For him whose children 'neath her zone she bare,
Who loved her once, now hate, as all may see.
What think ye is she?—a sea-snake, or a viper,
Whose touch blasts even him who 'scapes her fangs,
If reckless daring, venomous spite, can slay.
How shall I call this thing, and name aright?
A wild-beast snare?—the curtain of a bath
Muffling a dead man's feet?—O nay, a net!
Toils and foot-tangling vestures call thou these. 1000
Such thing as this some robber might possess
To trap the stranger, one that practiseth
A life of rapine, killing by this snare
Many, and makes his soul a forge of hell.
Never in mine home may such woman live
With me! God grant me childless death ere then!

CHORUS.

Alas for the piteous deed! Alas!
By a ghastly death thou hast been laid low;
And for him that remaineth alive is anguish flowerlike
    blooming.

ORESTES.

Wrought she that crime or no? My witness be 1010
This robe, incarnadined by Ægisthus' sword.
The dark blood-smear hath wrought with time's long
    lapse
To mar the dye-hues of the broidered work.
His praises now I speak, now wail his death,
Crying to this, my father's murder-web.
Deeds, sufferings I lament, yea, all mine house—
I, with this victory's loathed pollution stained!

CHORUS.

No man of the sons of earth shall pass
Through his whole life's journey unscathed of
　　woe.
Now is one disaster upon us: now near is a second
　　looming.　　　　　　　　　　　　　　1020

ORESTES.

Nay, know ye—for the end I cannot see—
As in a chariot-race I am swerving wide
Out of the course.　I am hurried helpless on
By reinless thoughts.　Upon my heart broods Fear
Ready to sing and dance her fury-dance!
But, ere my reason goes, I tell my friends—
Tell them, I slew my mother righteously,
The foul thing, loathed of Gods, that slew my sire.
He whose spells drew me to this deed, I claim,
Was Pytho's prophet Loxias, who foretold　　1030
That, doing it, I should be clear of blame;
Refraining—I name not the penalty :—
Some pangs outrange imagination's bow.
Now look on me, how, with this suppliant bough
And wreath arrayed, on earth's mid-navel stone
I shall sit down, on Loxias' holy floor,
By the altar-fire they name the Undying Flame,
Fleeing this taint of kindred blood :—no hearth
Save his alone, did Loxias bid me seek.
I bid all Argives in the days to be　　　　1040
Witness that not in cruelty I slew.
So I, a homeless wanderer from this land,
Living and dying leave this fame for mine.

CHORUS.

Nay, thou hast done well : yoke not thou thy lips
To words ill-omened : bode not horrors thou.
Freedom hast thou unto all Argos given,
Whose swift stroke lopped the heads of serpents twain.

ORESTES.

Ha !—Handmaid women, there in Gorgon guise
They come with sable robes and hair enwreathed
With tangled snakes ! I can no longer stay.   1050

CHORUS.

What fancies, O most duteous of all sons,
Rack thee ?   Stand firm—fear not, in victory's hour.

ORESTES.

No fancied shapes these my tormentors are !
These are my mother's hell-hounds manifest.

CHORUS.

Yet fresh-spilt is the blood upon thine hands ;
Therefrom distraction falleth on thy soul.

ORESTES.

O King Apollo ! lo, they swarm, they swarm !
The loathly blood is dripping from their eyes !

CHORUS.

Haste to where cleansing waits : to Loxias cling.
He from these agonies shall set thee free.   1060

ORESTES.

Ye, ye behold not these, but I behold !
I am hunted hence—I can no longer stay !

[Exit.

K

CHORUS.

Blessing go with thee!   God look graciously
On thee, and guard unto some happier lot!

Lo, how upon the palace royal hath burst
   The third storm that fulfils the house's fate!
First, wretch Thyestes at a feast accurst
      Of his own children ate:

Then shrieked the second storm the agony
   Of that king in that laver hacked to death,   1070
When the Achaians' chief to treachery
      There yielded up his breath:

Now on the third storm's wild wings down doth sweep
   A Saviour—or a Doom shall he be named?
Where shall the Curse end?—how be lulled to sleep
      Its fury?—how be tamed?

[Exeunt.

THE EUMENIDES
OR
THE RECONCILIATION.

ARGUMENT.

BECAUSE *Orestes had slain his mother, the Avengers of
Kindred Blood, the Spirits which are named Erinyes,
and Eumenides, and Furies, haunted him evermore,
chasing him from land to land. Though he had but
done the bidding of the Oracle of Apollo, and had
been purified, with all due rites, from the guilt of blood,
they would not be appeased, but pursued after him day
and night, with intent to wear and waste away his
life, and thereafter to torment him in death for ever.*

*And herein is told how he came to his last refuge,
and was set on his trial before the Powers of Heaven
and of Hell, and before men, and of the great propiti-
ation that was made.*

DRAMATIS PERSONÆ.

Apollo.

Athena.

Orestes, *son of Agamemnon and slayer of his mother.*

Ghost of Klytemnestra.

Priestess *of the Oracle at Delphi.*

The Judges, *twelve burghers of Athens.*

Chorus, *consisting of the twelve Eumenides, or Furies.*

Scene : 1st, the Temple of Apollo at Delphi.

       2nd, the Temple of Athena at Athens.

       3rd, the Areopagus at Athens.

THE EUMENIDES

OR

THE RECONCILIATION.

In front of the door of the temple.   Enter the Priestess.

PRIESTESS.

CHIEF place in this my prayer I give to Earth
First Prophetess; and unto Themis next,
Who second sat on this her mother's throne
Of prophecy, as saith the legend.   Third,
By her consent—constraint was none therein—
Phoebê, another Titan child of Earth,
Was throned thereon, and she her birth-gift gave
To Phœbus, who from Phœbê hath his name.
So left he Delos' mere and rocky ridge,
Landed on Pallas' ship-frequented shores,　　　　10
And came to this land, to Parnassus' shrine,
Whither the Fire-god's sons with reverent feet
Escorted him, the men that through the waste
His highway made, and tamed the savage earth.
So came he with high worship of our folk
And Delphos, king and helmsman of this land.
And Zeus with inspiration filled his soul,
And seated him fourth Prophet on the throne,
Loxias, interpreter of Father Zeus.

To these Gods I put up my prelude-prayer.   20
And Temple-warder Pallas hath mine homage.
The Nymphs I reverence, by Korykia's rock
Bird-loved that dwell, the caverned haunt of Gods.
And Bromius dwells here—I forget not him—
Since the God led his Bacchanals to war,
And to his doom snared Pentheus, like a hare.
On Pleistus' fountains, on Poseidon's might
I call, on Zeus most high, the Accomplisher.
So sit I down on my prophetic chair.
Vouchsafe ye me a better entrance now   30
Than all before !   What Greeks soe'er be here,
Let them by lot draw nigh, as custom bids :
For as the God guides, so I prophesy.

Enters the temple.   Comes tottering forth, clinging for
support to walls and pillars.

O dread to tell, O dread for eyes to see,
That which hath driven me back from Loxias' halls,
So strengthless that I cannot lift my steps,
Trailed by mine hands forth, sped not by my feet !
Age terror-thrilled is naught, is as a babe.
Into the crypt with garlands hung I passed—
There on the Navel-stone one god-accurst   40
I saw, in suppliant posture seated : blood
Dripped from his hands : a sword that seemed new-
        drawn
He grasped, and held an olive's topmost spray
All duly twined with wool-strands passing long
From snowy fleece :—my tale thus far is clear.
But lo, in front of this man a strange troop
Of women sleepeth on the chairs of stone—
Not women—Gorgons rather name I them ;

Yet not to Gorgon-shapes I liken these.
Once saw I pictured Harpies bearing off   50
The meat of Phineus—yet were these unwinged,
Swart-hued and hideous-wrought in every part.
Their breath out-snoring blasts whoe'er draw nigh;
And from their eyes drips down a loathly rheum.
Their vesture it were sacrilege to bring
Before Gods' statues, or to homes of men.
No tribe whence such a crew could spring I have seen,
Nor land that boasts, ' I have reared, uncursed thereby,
This brood, nor wailed disaster born of them.'
Let mighty Loxias, master of this fane,   60
Himself see to the issue of these things:
For he is Healer-prophet, Portent-seer,
Pollution-banisher even from others' homes.

*Scene opens, disclosing inner temple. Orestes clasping
omphalos. Furies sleeping.*

Enter Apollo and Hermes.

APOLLO.

I never will forsake thee.   To the end
I ward thee, standing nigh or far-withdrawn,
And to thy foes ungentle will I be.
Even now thou seest these ravin-demons trapped:
They are fallen on sleep, yon maidens all-abhorred,
Night's ancient children, with whom none of Gods
Hath commerce, no, nor ever man nor brute.   70
They are made for evil only, for they dwell
In evil gloom and nether Tartarus,
The hate of men and Gods Olympian.
Howbeit flee thou: let thy strength not fail;
For they will chase thee o'er far-stretching lands,

Ever as tramp the earth thy wandering feet,
And pass the sea and surf-ringed island-towns.
Yet faint not, thus, like some hard-driven steer,
On-goaded; but to Pallas' city go:
Clasping her ancient image seat thee there.   80
There will we find us judges of thy cause,
And words of suasion: so will we devise
Thy full deliverance from these sufferings,
For I, I thrust thee on to slay thy mother.

ORESTES.

O King Apollo, thou canst do no wrong;
And, being such, do thou forget me not.
Thy power is all-sufficient for mine aid.

APOLLO.

Remember: let not fear thine heart o'ercome.
And thou, my brother by the selfsame Sire,
Hermes, protect him.   To thy surname true[1]   90
Be guide to him : lead as a shepherd on
My suppliant.   Zeus respects that sanctity
Of outlaws, which thine escort lends to men.
            [Exeunt Apollo, Hermes, and Orestes.

*Ghost of Klytemnestra rises, and bends over the sleep-
ing Furies.*

KLYTEMNESTRA.

Ay, slumber on!   What do ye thus to sleep?
And I the while, thus set at nought of you,
Amidst the dead am made a laughing-stock,
A scorn of scorns, because of him I slew!

---

1. Hermes the Guide-god, as he is repeatedly called in Homer.

In shame I wander : yea, I tell you this,
That of the dead I am bitterly reviled.
Though nearest kin dealt me this hideous wrong, 100
None of the Gods is angered for my sake—
For me, butchered by matricidal hands !
Look on these stabs, in thine heart's vision look,
For in sleep lightened are the spirit's eyes :
By day the soul's prophetic gift doth fail.
Ha, oft have ye lapped up mine offerings,
Bowls—not of wine, but sober soothing gifts ;
Night-solemn feasts upon your hearth I burned
At such an hour as no God claims beside.
And all these see I trampled underfoot !   110
He hath 'scaped you ; like a fawn, clean gone is he,
Ay, lightly from the midst of these your toils
Hath sped, with curling lips of utter scorn.
Hearken to mine appeal for my soul's sake !
Give heed, O Goddesses of Nethergloom !
Klytemnestra calls you—now a bodiless dream !

Chorus mutter in sleep.

Ay, mutter on !   Your prey afar is fled !
Ha, friends hath he—not broken reeds like mine !

Chorus mutter in sleep.   120

O'er-sound thy sleep is—me thou pitiest not.
Gone is Orestes, slayer of his mother !

Chorus moan in sleep.

Thou moanest, slumberest—wilt not straightway rise ?
What hast thou ever done save fashion evil ?

Chorus moan in sleep.

Slumber and ache of toil, conspirators
Potent, have quelled the fearful dragon's **strength**.

Chorus break repeatedly into frenzied muttering.

CHORUS.

Seize, seize him, seize him, seize him! Ha, take
    heed!   130

KLYTEMNESTRA.

Chasing in dreams the prey—still giving tongue,
Like hound that ceaseth not to hunt in sleep!
What dost thou?—rise! Let toil not quell thy
    strength,
Let sleep not lull thee to forget my grief:
Let thy soul writhe beneath my just reproach,
For to the wise upbraidings are as goads.
Waft thou thy breath in spray of blood on him;
Blast him with fire-reek blazing from thy womb.
Chase—wither with pursuit renewed his strength.

Ghost descends.

The Furies one by one start up from sleep.

CHORUS.

Arouse—arouse thou her, as I rouse thee!   140
Ha! slumbering still?—arise!—spurn sleep from thee!
Let us see if this prelude peals in vain.

(Str. 1)

Woe for us! Out on it! Friends, with what anguish
    of toil have we wrought—
Manifold anguish endured, and have wasted our
    strength for nought—

Anguish and wrong unendurable !—Out on it ! well-
a-day !
Out of the toils hath he slipped; O, the quarry hath
stolen away !
Sleep-overcome was my vigilant watch—I have lost
the prey !

(Ant. 1)

Scion of Zeus, art a filcher, a thief !—ho, I taunt thee
with crime !
Youngling thou hast overridden divinities hoary as
time !—   150
Ay, hast regarded thy suppliant, the godless, unnatural son,
Stolen the matricide out of our clutch—this thy god-
head hath done !
Who shall stand up for thee—say that by justice this
vantage was won ?

(Str. 2)

Me the reproaches that burst through the midst of the
dreams of the night
Stung like a chariot-goad by the midst of the shaft
grasped tight ;
Ay, through mine heart and my liver I felt the ghost-
hand smite.
Writhing am I as one writhes 'neath the merciless
scourger's hand,
Lashed in the market-place by command of the lords
of the land,   160
Shivers and swoons, while the cold sweat-beads on his
white face stand.

(Ant. 2)

Such are the deeds that they do, these upstart gods of
an hour !

Such is their utter defiance of justice in using their
    power !
Lo, what a blood-clot, that drips with a very murder-
    shower,
Crimsons him, head to foot !—ye may see how the
    Navel-stone,
Pivot and centre of earth, is defiled, for thereover is
    thrown
Hideous pollution of bloodshed : the holy unholy is
    grown !

(Str. 3)

Prophet, thou surely hast taken the curse, whose
    pollution doth rest
Dark on that house ; on thy shrine hast thou thrust
    it, thine own bidden guest.   170
Contrariwise to the wont of the Gods thou regardest
    man,
Crushest the Fates which were born of old when time
    began.

(Ant. 3)

Yea, unto me is he tyrannous : yet shall he set him
    not free !
Ha, though he flee 'neath the earth, delivered he
    shall not be !
He, the polluted, shall find there another avenger of
    guilt
Waiting to wreak on his head the curse of the blood
    he hath spilt.

Enter Apollo.

APOLLO.

Out !   I command you, from these halls with speed
Depart—begone from my prophetic shrines,   180

Lest, feeling the winged flashing serpent's sting
As from the golden-plaited string it leaps,
Thou void for anguish black foam sucked from men,
Vomiting gouts of slaughter gorged by thee.
It fits not that ye touch these halls of mine.
Go where revenges cleave heads, gouge out eyes,
Where slaughters reek, where perisheth manhood's
    seed
From outraged boyhood's bloom, feet, hands, are
    lopped,
Where stones rain death, where long moans piteously
Burst from the wretch impaled :—ha, hear ye now 190
What festival, O demons god-abhorred,
Is your delight ? Therewith your form's whole fashion
Accordeth ! A blood-lapping lion's cave
Might such inhabit fitlier, not pollute
By your foul presence this my sanctuary.
Hence, beasts by keeper never shepherded !
Herd whereof none is pleasing to the Gods !

CHORUS.

O King Apollo, hearken thou in turn.
In this deed none with thee doth share the blame :
Thyself didst all ; the guilt is wholly thine.   200

APOLLO.

How, prithee ? Thus far lengthen out thy speech.

CHORUS.

Thine oracle made thy guest a matricide.

APOLLO.

Mine oracle bade avenge his sire—what then ?

CHORUS.

Thou promisedst shelter to him—red from murder!

APOLLO.

Yea, bade him flee for refuge to these halls.

CHORUS.

And us, who dogged him hither, dost revile?

APOLLO.

Yea, for mine house is not for you to approach.

CHORUS.

But our appointed work, our right, is this.

APOLLO.

Your rights?—ay, vaunt your high prerogative!

CHORUS.

We chase the mother-slayers from their homes.   210

APOLLO.

What of the wife that murdereth her lord?

CHORUS.

That is no blood of kin by kindred shed.

APOLLO.

Lo, thou dishonourest, hold'st as nothing-worth,
The troth that Hera hallowed, wedding Zeus.
An outcast by thy plea is Kypris made,
Of whom the ties most dear to mortals spring.
For marriage fate-ordained for man and wife,
Warded by Justice, mightier is than oaths.
And if thou slack thine hand from punishing

When these their yokemates slay, nor look in wrath,
Wrongfully, say I, dost thou hunt Orestes.   [220
Against this sin I mark thee fiercely rage,
By that unruffled, all the world may see.
But Goddess Pallas shall see justice done.

CHORUS.

Ne'er will I cease from haunting yonder man!

APOLLO.

O yea, pursue!—so get to thee more toil.

CHORUS.

Curtail not thou mine honours by thy speech!

APOLLO.

Thine honours!—as a gift not mine be they!

CHORUS.

O **yea,** great art thou named by Zeus's throne!
But I—for a mother's blood aye draws me on—   230
Claim him for punishment, still hunt him down.

APOLLO.

But I will shield and save my suppliant.
For men and Gods account a fearful thing
The wrath of suppliants wilfully betrayed.

*Scene changes to Temple of Athena at Athens.   Orestes
discovered clinging to her statue.*

ORESTES.

Athena, Queen, by Loxias' commands
I come.   Be gracious to a hunted wretch,
Whose stain is not unpurged from hands uncleansed,

But dulled by now, yea, vesture-like worn thin
By touch of homes and paths of other men.
Far-journeying alike o'er land and sea,　　　　　240
Heeding the hests of Loxias' oracles,
Goddess, thine house, thine image, have I reached;
And here, till Justice speak my doom, I wait.

Enter Chorus.

CHORUS.

Ha! lo you there, the man's slot plain to see!
Follow the tokens of the voiceless guide!
For, as the hound pursues the wounded fawn,
By blood-spot and by foam-fleck track we him.
With manifold strength-outwearing toil hard pants
Mine heart; for all earth have we quested o'er,
And o'er the sea with wingless hoverings　　　　　250
I came pursuing, by no ship outsped.
And now he cowereth somewhere hidden nigh.
Ha! blithely it greets me—scent of human blood!
　　　Watch, O watch with sleepless care,
　　　Peering here and glancing there,
　　　Lest the unpunished matricide
　　　Flee by speed, by cunning hide.
　　　Lo there once more!—protection hath he found!
　　　Clasping the immortal Goddess' image round
　　　He claims the right of trial of his guilt.　　　260
　　　This may not be: a mother's life-blood spilt
　　　On earth, may not be gathered up again:
　　　'Tis past recall, once poured upon the plain.
Nay, I shall suck—thou canst not choose but pay the
　　　penalty—
The red gore from thy living limbs, and win me out
　　　of thee

The banquet of a draught that shall with awful
    anguish flow.
Yea, I will waste thy living frame, then drag thee far
    below,
There to pay all thy penalty, the mother-murderer's
    woe.
      So shall all else that have transgressed,
      Have sinned against a God, a guest,   270
      Or parents, mark how each receives
      The dues of sin that Justice gives.
   For Hades 'neath the earth waits every soul,
   A mighty judge who watcheth to enscroll
   All sins on his eternal memory's roll.

ORESTES.

I, lessoned in misfortune's school, have learnt
Full many a cleansing rite, have learnt when Law
Requireth speech, or silence ; and herein
By a wise teacher's bidding do I speak.
Lo, the blood sleeps and fades upon mine hand,   280
And matricide's pollution is washed clean.
For, when it yet was fresh, at Phœbus' hearth
'Twas banished by ablutions of slain swine.
Long were the tale, from its beginning told,
Of all I have visited, nor brought them harm.
Time cleanseth all things, aging as they age.
And now with pure lips piously I call
Upon Athena, this land's Queen, to come
Mine helper : so without war shall she win
Myself, my land, and Argos' folk, for hers,   290
Her loyal ally ever, by just right.
Be she in regions of far Libya-land
By Triton's flow, the stream that gave her birth,

Erect, or throned with vesture-veilèd foot,
Armed for friends' aid, or over Phlegra's plain
Like some bold captain darts she an eagle-glance—
Let her, as Goddess, hear from far, and come,
Come, to be my deliverer from these ills.

CHORUS.

Thee nor Apollo, nor Athena's might
Shall save from perishing, an outcast thing,   300
A soul that hath forgot the taste of joy,
A prey by fiends sucked bloodless, a thin wraith ! . . . .
Dost thou reply not ?　Dost thou spurn my words ?—
Thou, for me nourished, unto me devoted ?
Slain on no altar, thou shalt feast me alive,
Shalt hear the hymn that charms thee by this spell :—

     Sisters, weave we now the dance :
     Now 'tis time to chant our song,
     Chant the ghastly doom of wrong :
     Publish now the ordinance   310
     This our band for men doth frame :—
     We unbending justice claim.
     They whose hands no guilt imbrues,
     No such men our wrath pursues ;
     Scatheless on through life they win.
     When they, like this man of sin,
     Cover hands that murders stain,
     Righteous champions of the slain,
     Blood-avengers, we attend,
     Haunting them unto the end.   320

(Str. 1)

Mother, who didst bear me, Mother Night, a venge-
    ance ever near

Unto men bereft of life-light, men yet seeing light, O
　　hear!
Me the son of Leto doth dishonour, from mine hands
　　would fain
Wrest this cowerer, mine atonement-victim for a
　　mother slain!
Ha, but o'er our slaughtered[1] victim hear our chant
　　triumphant ring!—
Madness, frenzy soul-destroying, is the hymn the
　　Erinyes sing,　　　　　　　　　　　　　　　　330
Soul-enchaining, lyreless, blasting mortal frames and
　　withering!

(Ant. 1)

This our lot and portion is, the thread by Doom the
　　unswerving spun
For our sure prerogative—that mortals by whose
　　hands are done
Impious murders, aye we haunt them till they sink
　　into the grave.
Yea, and 'neath the earth our bondmen are they: none
　　shall help nor save.　　　　　　　　　　　　340
Ay, and o'er our slaughtered victim hear our chant
　　triumphant ring!—
Madness, frenzy soul-destroying, is the hymn the
　　Erinyes sing,
Soul-enchaining, lyreless, blasting mortal frames and
　　withering.

(Str. 2)

　In the hour that beheld our being begun
　　Were these our prerogatives ratified:

1.　Proleptic, as in ' So these two brothers and *their murdered
man* rode to fair Florence.'　(Keats, *Pot of Basil.*)

No dealings have we with Immortals ; none		350
  Will deign at the banquet to sit by our side :
No part nor lot for ever have I
In white robes' glistering radiancy ;
But we take for our portion the desolation
Of homes which are made Strife's habitation :
  When the hand is with life-blood of kin made red,
Then hunt we the slayer ; our strength shall out-
    last him,
Be he never so swift ; we o'ertake him, we blast
    him
  By the power of the blood ever-fresh he hath shed.
                      (Ant. 2)

And we give all diligence hereunto		360
  That our burden shall be from the Gods afar
Removed, that the vengeance-quest be our due,
  That the kin-slayer stand not before their bar.
  The blood-streaming abhorred ones doth Zeus
    disallow ;
  He hears not their prayer, he rejecteth their vow.
Then we, from our ambush of cloud down-flashing,
With a leap as of lions bring down the crashing
  Might of our feet on the wretch as he flies,
With the clutch of our talons to earthward flinging
The limbs that the strength of terror is winging—
  Lo, crushed under ruin resistless he lies !		[370
                      (Str. 3)

Imaginations proudly swelling of men beneath the free
    sky dwelling
  Deep under earth shall shrivel shame-abased,
Soon as our onrush shall have found them, soon as
    our black robes sweep around them
  In measures that our vengeful feet have paced.

(Ant. 3)
The wretch sin-wildered falls, unknowing whence
    comes his sudden overthrowing,
    Above him drifts such pestilence of gloom,
While voices multitudinous-groaning their wrongs
    against his house are moaning,   [380
    Whose breath is blackness of the mist of doom.
(Str. 4)
Law abideth everlasting : cunning are we, and unfail-
    ing
Workers of its sentence, awful sin-recorders : un-
    availing
        With us is prayer.
Onward ever press we hasting to perform an office
    lacking
Honour, worship—yea, unlawful for the Gods
    Olympian—tracking
        Paths of despair
Down through sunless darkness sloping : stumbling
    blindly, blindly groping
Sinners unbereft of sight, sinners death-bereft of light
        Wander there.
(Ant. 4)
Who of mortals doth not shiver all his pulses through,
    and feareth
For the terror of my coming, when the awful law he
    heareth,   390
        Mine ordinance ?—mine
By decrees of Fate for ever sealed and ratified, and
    given
Into these, the Hands of Dooming working out the
    will of Heaven,
        The law divine ?—

Such my right from times eternal : none may scorn
    me, though infernal
Darkness brood above the place assigned to me, where
    never rays
        Of sun may shine.

Athena descends.

ATHENA.

From far, beside Skamander, thine appeal
I heard, where I took seisin of the land,
Even that which the Achaian chiefs and kings
Assigned for ever, root and fruit, to me,   400
My goodly portion of the spoils of war,
A gift for Theseus' scions set apart.
Thence came I, onward speeding tireless feet :
The winds, my viewless car-steeds, flew so fast
That in their wingless flight mine ægis hissed.
Seeing this concourse, wholly strange to earth,
I fear not, yet amazement fills mine eyes.
Who, who be ye ?—to all your rout I speak,
And to this stranger by mine image crouched.
Speak, ye who are like to none of all earth's seed, 410
Who are not of Goddesses whom Gods behold,
Who bear no semblance unto human shape—
Yet it beseems not that bystanders mock
A shape deform : justice draws back therefrom.

CHORUS.

Daughter of Zeus, thou shalt in brief learn all.
Children are we of everlasting Night.
The Curses are we named in the Underworld.

ATHENA.

Thy lineage now I know, thy name and fame.

CHORUS.

Yea, straight shalt thou learn my prerogatives.

ATHENA.

Fain would I, if they may be plainly told.   420

CHORUS.

Slayers of men we chase forth from their homes.

ATHENA.

What bourne hath the manslayer's banishment?

CHORUS.

Where happiness hath nowhere any place.

ATHENA.

Such exile dost thou hiss against yon man?

CHORUS.

Yea, for he took on him to slay his mother.

ATHENA.

Fear-spurred by no strong Power, no wrath of
Heaven?

CHORUS.

What goad so keen as spur to matricide?

ATHENA.

Before the court are two pleas—one is heard.

CHORUS.

Nay, he would neither take nor tender oath.[1]

---

1. *i.e.* He will not comply with the formalities of procedure,
and therefore I demand that he be at once non-suited.

ATHENA.

More than her deeds thou lovest Justice' name. 430

CHORUS.

How?—teach me: wisdom hast thou and to spare.

ATHENA.

I say, no oaths can make the wrong prevail.

CHORUS.

Made inquisition then ; judge righteous judgment.

ATHENA.

Commit ye this decision unto me ?

CHORUS.

Yea surely, worthy child of worthy sire.

ATHENA.

Stranger, in thy turn what wilt say hereto ?
Thy land, thy lineage, thine afflictions tell
First ; then repel thou thine accusers' charge,
If thou in justice trusting hast sat down
Clasping mine image, hard beside mine hearth, 440
A sacred suppliant, as Ixion sat.
Answer all this, and be thine answer clear.

ORESTES.

Athena, Queen, the dark misgiving first
That lurks in thy last words, I do away.
I am not guilt-stained : no pollution comes
From mine hand, by thine image as I crouch.
And I will give thee perfect proof of this :—
Sealed are the tainted murderer's lips by law,
Till by the blood-atoning minister

A suckling beast's blood have besprent his hands. 450
Long since in other fanes thus purified
Was I, by victims and by running streams.
So I pronounce this fear clean put away.
Now of my lineage straightway shalt thou hear.
An Argive am I: well thou know'st my sire,
Agamemnon, marshaller of sea-borne men,
With whom thou madest Ilium's city Troy
No city.   He at his home-coming died
Shamefully.   Yea, my mother, the black-souled,
Slew him : she shrouded him in subtle toils   460
Which witness still that murder of the bath.
When I, an exile theretofore, came home,
I slew my mother, I deny it not,
In vengeance for mine own dear father's blood.
What guilt is in this deed doth Loxias share,
Who threatened pangs, to sting mine heart as goads,
If on the guilty I wreaked no revenge.
Thou judge my deed ; pronounce it right or wrong ;
Howe'er thou deal with me, I murmur not.

ATHENA.

The matter is so great, no mortal man   470
Dare judge it.   I, even I, am disallowed
From giving doom on vengeance-waking murder ;
The more, since thou hast been assoiled, and yet,
Though shriven and clean, cam'st suppliant to my
     fane.
Howbeit, as purged, I bid thee enter Athens.
Yet these—their dues not lightly are set aside ;
And, if their cause be not victorious,
The venom of their malice shall thereafter
Fall on the land in plagues intolerable.

Thus stands it—whether they depart or stay   480
Alike is grievous : I am in a strait.
But, seeing this bolt from out the blue falls here,
Sworn judges will I choose of murder, so
An ordinance for ever will ordain.
Ye, summon your sworn witnesses, and show
Proofs, by the which shall justice be maintained.
The best of all my burghers will I choose,
And come, that these may truly try this cause,
Oath-bound to utter no unrighteous verdict.

> *[Exeunt Athena and Oréstes.*

CHORUS.   *(Str. 1)*

Now shall be overthrown the old-time laws,   490
    New statutes shall bear sway,
If yonder mother-murderer's cause, the cause
    Of wrong, prevail this day.
Lo, this day's work shall arm full many an one
    With reckless lust of crime ;
For many a parent murdered by a son
Doth veriest agony wait—nor now alone,
    But through all tides of time.

(Ant. 1)

The Frenzied Furies, who mankind behold,
    No more shall curse this sin,   500
But slip the leash of murders manifold
    Of kin by hands of kin.
Man shall ask man, the while he tells the tale
    Of wrongs to near kin wrought,
'How shall these plagues end—cease awhile to assail ?'
Ah wretch ! his comfort shall no whit avail,
    His cure shall profit nought.

(*Str.* 2)

Ha! then let none appeal when his days darken,
    When murder's dagger smites,   510
Crying to heaven his prayer—'Hear, Justice!—
   hearken,
    Thrones of the Avenging Sprites!'
Thus may a father from death's anguish calling
    Shriek, or a mother slain—
Too late! This day is Justice' temple falling:
    Tears build it not again.

(*Ant.* 2)

'Tis good that Fear yet lingering midst the nations
    Somewhere should watch man's soul
Throned in the conscience, good that tribulations
    Should teach men self-control.   520
Who, if he nurture not a spirit humble,
    When all his path is bright,
Who—be it state or man—can choose but stumble
    From reverence for Right?

(*Str.* 3)

Envy not thou the freedom that defieth
Control, nor that slave-life which cowering lieth
    A tyrant lord's footstool:
'*God to life's middle walk the palm hath given
Aye*'—though elsewhere the governance of Heaven
    Seem ordered by no rule—   530
Ay, and my strain this chord with that inweaveth:
'*Verily godlessness, when it conceiveth,
    Brings arrogance to birth;*'
But child of wholesome soberness of spirit
Fair fortune is, which all men pray to inherit,
    Dear to all sons of earth.

(Ant. 3)
This of my teaching is the sum—O hear it !—
Justice's altar, see that thou revere it :
    Dare not spurn this aside   [540
With godless heel, what time thy passions blind thee
To all save gain : vengeance is close behind thee ;
    Fixed doth the end abide.
Then, whosoe'er thou art, with reverence lowly
Honour thy father and thy mother : holy
    Be in thy sight the claim
Of him who cometh to thy portals faring
Thy guest ; with hospitality unsparing
    Do thou receive the same.

(Str. 4)
    He who of his free will   550
    Doth righteousness, shall still
    Be blest : no surge of ill
        Shall whelm him under :
    But he who overleaps
    Justice, whose dragnet sweeps
    In heaps confused on heaps
        Unhallowed plunder,
    He shall perforce at last
    Lower his sail, when mast
    And yard by trouble's blast
        Are riven asunder.

(Ant. 4)
    He, shrieking forth his prayer
    To heavens that hear not, there
    Mid whirlpits of despair
        Hellward descendeth.
    God laughs at him, to see   560
    His helpless agony—

Fool, who made boast, ' O'er me
No doom impendeth ! '
Hurled toward yon ness his keel
O'er Justice' reef doth reel—
Lost, lost, unwept, his weal
For ever endeth !

*The scene changes to the Areopagus at Athens. Enter
Athena, with twelve Athenian burghers. Then
enter Orestes, followed by the Chorus.*

ATHENA.

Herald, lift up thy voice ; hush thou the throng ;
And let the shattering Tuscan trumpet's throat,
Filled with the straining breath of mortal lips,
Peal forth its cry far-soaring o'er the host.
While filling are these judgment-seats, it fits   570
That men be hushed, that all the city hear
Mine ordinance eternal, that this man
May hear withal, and justice' doom be given.
      [Trumpet. Enter Apollo.

CHORUS.

Apollo, King, thou lord it o'er thine own !
Say thou, what hast thou with this cause to do ?

APOLLO.

I come to bear my witness : this man is
Guest of my temple, suppliant of my shrine.
And I am he that cleansed this murder-stain,
And I am he shall justify him.   Mine
The guilt is of this mother's murder.   Thou   580
Open this cause, and, as thou find'st, decide.

ATHENA *(to Chorus.)*

First word to you: I open so this cause;
For right it is that first the accuser speak,
From the beginning setting forth the matter.

CHORUS.

Many we are, yet shall our words be few.
Thou, answering, by each question set reply.
Thy mother—tell us first, didst thou slay her?

ORESTES.

I slew: ,not on denial rests my plea.

CHORUS.

Lo, of the three falls one already ours!

ORESTES.

Thou vauntest over one not thrown as yet.   590

CHORUS.

Nay, thou must tell how thou didst murder her.

ORESTES.

I tell: mine hand drew sword and gashed her throat.

CHORUS.

So?—moved of whom, and by whose counselling?

ORESTES,

By this God's oracles.   He my witness is.

CHORUS.

He, the God-prophet, bade thee slay thy mother!

ORESTES.

He: nor thus far I murmur at my fate.

CHORUS.

Doomed by the votes, thou soon shalt change thy tone !

ORESTES.

I trust yet.   My sire helps me from his tomb.

CHORUS.

O yea, trust in the dead, thou mother-slayer !

ORESTES.

Yea, for a twofold crime polluted her.   600

CHORUS.

Yea ?—how ?   Instruct these judges touching this.

ORESTES.

She slew her husband, and she slew my sire.

CHORUS.

Death, then, her debt hath cancelled, not thine—yet.

ORESTES.

Why did ye hunt not *her*, while yet she lived ?

CHORUS.

She was not blood-kin to the man she slew.

ORESTES.

And I, am I by blood my mother's kin ?

CHORUS.

Bare she not thee, red murderer, 'neath her zone ?
Dar'st thou disown thy mother's most dear blood ?

ORESTES.

Now bear thou witness.   Set thou forth for me,

Apollo, if I slew her rightfully.	610
For I disown the deed not, as it stands.
If rightly shed or wrongly seems this blood
To thy mind, judge, that I may tell it these.

APOLLO.

To you, Athena's great court, will I speak
Righteously.   I, the Prophet, will not lie.
Never I spake on my prophetic throne
Concerning man, nor woman, neither state,
Aught save what Zeus the Olympians' Father bade.
Heed ye the might of this, the Fount of Justice,
And bow before the purpose of my Sire;	620
No oath prevails to override Zeus' word.

CHORUS.

Zeus, as thou sayest, gave this oracle
That bade Orestes for his sire's blood take
Vengeance, and count as nought his mother's right!

APOLLO.

Is *her* death like a highborn hero's death,
One honoured with the sceptre Zeus bestowed ?—
And he by a woman slain—not with fierce shafts
That smite from far, as of some Amazon;
But as thou, Pallas, shalt be told, and ye
That sit to give your judgment-vote hereon.	630
Home from the war, from earning meed of glory
Beyond all other, she with loyal words
Welcomed him : as he bathed, she cast o'er him
Tent-like a robe that overdraped all ; smote
Her lord so trammelled in the gapless shroud.
This doom, as hath been told, that hero found,
The worship-worthy lord of sea-borne hosts.

So paint I her, that indignation-stung
May be all folk ordained to judge this cause.

Chorus.

Zeus, by thy tale, most heeds the father's fate :   640
Yet himself fettered Kronos, his grey sire !
How dar'st thou say this clashes not with that ?
Judges, I call you to record—give ear !

Apollo.

O monsters all-abhorred, things loathed of Gods !
Fetters might one loose: this wrong may be healed ;
Yea, many a device to 'scape there is.
But when the dust hath drunk the blood of man,
Once dead, no resurrection is there then.
For this my sire hath wrought no healing-spell,
Though all things else he can reverse and change 650
At will, in no wise panting in his strength.

Chorus.

Nay, mark whereunto tends thy plea for him :
Who poured his mother's blood—his own—to earth,
Shall *he* in Argos in his sire's halls dwell
Thereafter?—at what public altars pray ?
What clansmen's lustral laver shall receive him ?

Apollo.

This answer I—my pleading's justice mark !
The mother of the child named hers is not
The parent, but the new-sown issue's nurse.
The sire is parent ; she but harboureth,   660
A stranger-guest, such life as God blasts not.
Lo, of mine argument I give you proof :—
There may be father without mother.   There,

Child of Olympian Zeus, the witness stands;
Not fostered she in darkness of the womb,
Yet scion such as Goddess never bare.
'Pallas, in all else to mine utmost power
Will I make great thy city and thy folk;
And this man to thy temple-hearth I sent
That he might be your leal friend evermore,   670
That thou mightst win him, Goddess, your ally,
Him and his children, and that by the seed
Of these this covenant may be cherished aye.

ATHENA *(to Chorus).*

Shall I bid these men from their conscience now
Judge righteous judgment ?—Hath enough been said ?

CHORUS.

Yea, for our every shaft by this is shot.
I wait to hear how shall the cause be judged.

ATHENA *(to Apollo and Orestes.)*

How then ? are ye content that so I rule ?

APOLLO.

Ye have heard whom ye have heard: now in your
      hearts
Respect your oath the while ye give the vote.   680

ATHENA.

Now hearken to the statute, Attic folk
Who judge this first of trials for shed blood.
Yea, and henceforth for Aigeus' people stands
This council-place of judges evermore;
Here on the War-God's Hill, the Amazons' camp
Where stood their tents,when came their host for hate

Of Theseus, and against yon town uppiled,
New-reared with stately towers, their rival burg,
And sacrificed to Ares, whence the rock
Is named the War-God's Hill:—here Reverence 690
With Fear her sister, homed in burghers' hearts
By day and night, shall all wrong-doing curb,
While my folk take them not new laws for old:
But if with tainted inflow and with mire
Thou foul clear water, thou canst drink not thence.
I warn my burghers—neither anarchy
Nor tyranny embrace ye nor revere,
Nor yet cast ye all fear beyond your walls:
For what man can be just who feareth nought?
In righteous awe of this court's majesty   700
Such bulwark of your land and of your town,
Such safeguard, shall ye find, as no folk hath
From norland Scythia south to Pelops' realm.
This judgment-court do I thus found, by bribes
Untainted, awful, unto vengeance swift,
A warder watching o'er a sleeping land.
This exhortation have I lengthened out
Unto my burghers for all time.   Now rise,
Take each his pebble, and determine right
In reverence for your oath.   My say is said.   710

CHORUS.

Lo now, I warn you in no wise to slight
Us, heavy-handed visitants of your land.

APOLLO.

And I command you, fear mine oracles,
That are of Zeus too: fruitless make them not.

CHORUS.

Thou dost usurp this cognisance of blood !
No more shall be thine oracles undefiled.

APOLLO.

How ?—erred Allfather in his counsels, when
Ixion the first murderer suppliant came ?

CHORUS.

Ay, talk !   If justice be denied to me,
I for its ruin haunt henceforth this land.   720

APOLLO.

Tush ! amid new and olden Gods alike
Thou art unhonoured.   Victory shall be mine.

CHORUS.

In Pheres' halls so didst thou—didst persuade
The Fates to grant men immortality.

APOLLO.

Was it not right to bless who reverenced me,
In that hour most when sorest was his need ?

CHORUS.

The old order thou destroyedst, and with wine
Didst thou beguile the Ancient Goddesses.

APOLLO.

Soon shalt thou, by the judgment's issue foiled,
Spue forth thy venom, yet harm not thy foes.   730

CHORUS.

Since thou, the young, o'erridest me the old,
Only to hear the sentence given I wait,
Yet doubtful whether to be wroth with Athens.

ATHENA.

With me it rests to give my sentence last.
I to Orestes' cause shall add this vote :
For mother is there none that gave me birth :
I am wholly—save for marriage—with the male
With all my soul ; I take the father's side.
Of so much less account I hold the death
Of her who slew her lord, the household's head. 740
If equal be the votes, Orestes wins.
Cast forth the lots with all speed from the urns
Ye judges unto whom this office falls.

ORESTES.

Phœbus Apollo, how shall this strife end ?

CHORUS.

O Night, dark mother, seest thou these things ?

ORESTES.

Now strangling waits for me, or light of life !

CHORUS.

Ruin for us, or dignities increased !

APOLLO.

Mine hosts, the votes cast forth count ye aright :
Justice in your decision reverence ye.
If one vote lack, comes great calamity,   750
And one vote rightly cast redeems a house.

ATHENA.

Acquitted is this man for blood arraigned ;
For equal is the tale of either votes.

ORESTES.

O Pallas, O thou saviour of mine house,
I was bereft of fatherland, and thou
Restoredst me !   Now many a Greek shall say :
' Argive once more, the man mid wealth ancestral
May dwell, by grace of Pallas, Loxias,
And of that third, the Saviour-lord, who rules
All things,' who for my sire's fate had respect,   760
Who, seeing these, the Avengers, saves me now.
And I unto this land and to thy folk
Make oath, as homeward now I turn to go,
That henceforth, through the fulness of all time,
Hitherward never chieftain of my land
Marching shall raise the battle-marshalled spear ;
For I myself then lying in my tomb,
Will make their march, if they transgress this oath,
By irresistible calamities
Dark with despair, their voyaging accurst,   770
So that they shall repent them of their toil.
If mine oath rest inviolate, I will be
All-gracious to them while they honour aye
This burg of Pallas with confederate spear.
Farewell : mayst thou and these that ward thy walls,
Grappling with foes, find none to 'scape your might,
Your conquering spear whereon deliverance rides.

[Exit with Apollo.

CHORUS.   *(Str. 1)*

Upstart Gods, ye have downridden
  Olden laws, have left mine hand
Void !   Oh misery !—I am bidden   780
  Yield mine honours !   This your land
  Under my wrath lies banned :

I avenge my grief by casting
  Venom-spray thereon, the spume
Frothing from mine heart, and blasting
  Tree disleafed and barren womb.
    The crushed land's canker-doom—
Ho for Justice!—lo, is raining
  Ruin-drops on grass and corn !
What should I do else?—tamely plaining
Bear mocks?—not visit their disdaining   790
    On this people ? Ah forlorn
      Daughters whom Night hath borne,
        Now things of scorn !

ATHENA.

Give heed to me : groan not so heavily.
Ye are not vanquished. Nay, by equal votes
Fairly was sentence passed. Ye are not slighted.
Nay, but from Zeus clear testimony came—
And who revealed it, also testified—
' Of this deed let Orestes take no hurt.'
Therefore let not your anger's lightning smite   800
This land, nor nurse ye wrath, nor blast the fruits
Thereof by down-dropt gouts of demon-spite—
Relentless darts devouring seeds of life.
For here in utter faith I promise you
Shrines, sanctuary-crypts in a just land—
Where by your hearths shall ye sit splendour-
    throned,—
To have and hold, aye honoured by my folk.

CHORUS.   *(Ant. 1)*

Upstart Gods, ye have downridden
  Olden laws, have left mine hand

Void !   Oh misery !—I am bidden   810
   Yield mine honours !   This your land
    Under my wrath lies banned :
I avenge my grief by casting
   Venom-spray thereon, the spume
Frothing from mine heart, and blasting
   Tree disleafed and barren womb.
    The crushed land's canker-doom—
Ho for Justice !—lo, is raining
   Ruin-drops on grass and corn !
What should I do else ?—tamely plaining
Bear mocks ?—not visit their disdaining   820
   On this people ?   Ah forlorn
    Daughters whom Night hath borne,
    Now things of scorn !

ATHENA.

Ye are not dishonoured.   Do not in fell wrath,
Goddesses, smite past healing mortals' land.
I too in Zeus trust,—yet why speak hereof?—
And know, alone of Gods, the keys that ward
The chamber where his thunderbolts are sealed :—
Nay, but such arms I need not !   Swayed by me,
Cast not the fruitage of a froward tongue   830
Earthward, to blast all increase of the land.
Lull thou this storm-black billow's bitter rage
As one with me that dwells, with awe revered.
When thine the firstfruits are of sacrifice
For babes and wedlock-rites through this wide land
For ever, this my counsel shall ye praise.

CHORUS.   *(Str. 2)*

O that I thus should be dealt with !—'neath earth to
   be banished, be banished !

I, with the wisdom of old who am dowered, shall I
    dwell with you, I,
Held a pollution, an outcast whose honour hath
    vanished, hath vanished?
Nay, but I breathe out all fury, all wrath—Earth,
    hearken my cry!   840
Ah for the thrill of the pang through mine heart that
    is stinging, is stinging!
Bow down thine ear to the cry of mine anger, my
    mother, O Night!
Cunning resistless of Gods from my grasp hath been
    wringing—yea, wringing
As from a thing of nought—mine immemorial right!

ATHENA.

Still with thy wrath I bear—the elder thou,
And wiser far than I in manifold lore:
Yet prudent wit to me too Zeus hath given.   850
Now if to an alien land ye hence depart,
For my land shall ye pine; this I foretell.
The forward-flowing tide of time shall be
Richer in blessing to my folk; and thou,
Enthroned in honour mid Erechtheus' homes,
Shalt win such homage from his sons and daughters
As never shalt thou have of other men.[1]   857
Such blessings from mine hand thou mayest choose,
Doing, receiving good, with honour high   [867
My partner in this god-beloved land.

CHORUS.   *(Ant. 2)*

O that I thus should be dealt with!—'neath earth to
    be banished, be banished!   870

1. Weil's transference of the next nine lines to follow l. 912
is here adopted.

I, with the wisdom of old who am dowered, shall I
    dwell with you, I,
Held a pollution, an outcast whose honour hath
    vanished, hath vanished?
Nay, but I breathe out all fury, all wrath—Earth,
    hearken my cry!
Ah for the thrill of the pang through mine heart that
    is stinging, is stinging!
Bow down thine ear to the cry of mine anger, my
    mother, O Night!
Cunning resistless of Gods from my grasp hath been
    wringing—yea, wringing   [880
As from a thing of nought—mine immemorial right!

ATHENA.

I will not weary of fair speech to thee.
Ne'er shalt thou say that thou, the elder god,
By me, the younger, and by Athens' folk
Wast driven dishonoured forth to banishment.
If holy thou account the majesty
Of Suasion, and the peace-spell of my tongue,
O then remain.   If thou wilt not remain,
Wrongfully shalt thou hurl against my town
Wrath, rancorous spite, or scathe unto her sons.
Lo, thine it is to hold this land in fee   890
By lawful right in honour evermore.

CHORUS.

Athena, Queen, thou tell'st me of a home?—

ATHENA.

Unvexed of all annoy.   Accept thou this.

CHORUS.

Grant I accept—what honour waiteth me?

ATHENA.

That no house shall without thy blessing thrive.

CHORUS.

Wilt thou make sure that I shall have such power ?

ATHENA.

Yea, I will prosper such as reverence thee.

CHORUS.

Wilt thou for all time plight thy troth hereto ?

ATHENA.

What I will not fulfil I need not say.

CHORUS.

Meseems thy words bring balm—mine anger dies. 900

ATHENA.

Dwell in the land, and thou shalt get thee friends.

CHORUS.

What hymn wouldst thou that I chant o'er the land ?

ATHENA.

A hymn that hails a glorious victory's dawn,
A hymn of boons from earth, from ocean's dew,
From heaven, invoking breathings of the winds
To waft the sun-gold as they pace the land ;
A hymn of earth's increase, of flocks and herds
Abounding, failing never with the years,
A hymn of babes in kindly travail born.
But be thou strict to root the impious out,   910
Our weeds—for as a gardener cherish I
And shield from sorrow's blight the righteous race.

[Hurl thou not o'er my land the seeds of strife,　858
Whetstones of blood, whereof brave hearts are pierced
Frenzied with passion kindled not with wine.
Nor, plucking forth the fierce cock's fiery heart,
In my folk plant it, kindling civic broil
Of brothers against brothers ranged defiant.
Be their wars all with aliens—wars enow
For hearts wherein stern lust of glory burns !—
But of the home-bird's bickerings will I none.]　866
Such boons be thine : but in the glorious strife
Of war, myself will suffer not this town
To be uncrowned with victory midst the nations.

CHORUS.　　　　　　(Str. 1)

I accept : for mine home no more I refuse
　　　Queen Pallas's dwelling.
I will wrong not the city which most high Zeus
　　　And the War-god, excelling
In strength, have accounted their fortress-town ;
　　　For she, to deliver
Gods' altars from spoilers shall battle, their crown
　　　Of rejoicing for ever.　　　　　　920
I call down blessing on her in this hour,
　　　In love foretelling
How the sun with his quickening splendour shall
　　shower
Wealth on her, life's fullest bliss for her dower
　　　As a fountain upwelling.

ATHENA.

　All this hath my love's zeal done
　For my people : a home have I given
In their midst to the Mighty Ones hard to be won,

Yea, to them from whose lordship exempted is none
  Of mortals under the heaven.   [930
    Who hath felt not their power knoweth not
    Whence calamity comes in his lot.
Him sins long past in their chains bind fast,
  And hale him their bar before;
And by silent Death is his clamorous breath
    Stilled evermore.

CHORUS.   (Ant. 1)

O the boons that I chant, they are mine to bestow!
    No blight breathe, flinging
Death-dews on the trees, nor the sun's fierce glow
    Shrivel buds at their springing   940
Or ever they break from the cradle-sheath
    Of their wintertide-sleeping.
No rust touch the corn with its cancerous teeth
    Like a serpent on-creeping.
By the bounty of Pan twin lambs let the ewe
    Ever bear, as on-winging
The hours lead hither the year born anew:
So thy land of its treasure-trove yearly their due
    To the Gods shall be bringing.

ATHENA.

  Ho, warders of my wall,
  Hear ye their blessings?—all
  These surely shall befall;   950
    For all-prevailing
  The mighty Erinnys is
  With Gods aye throned in bliss,
  With Dwellers in the Abyss.
    Clear-seen, unfailing,

Man's cup of doom they brim ;
And some lives one glad hymn
Make they, some misty-dim
  With tears of wailing.

CHORUS.   *(Str. 2)*

And I ban the arrow that darkling flieth,
    Whereby man dieth
    Before his hour.
Unto sweet maids ope ye the new life's portals
    Of love, Immortals
    Who hold this power.   960
O Fates, our sisters, O strict dividers
    Of doom, abiders
    In every home
With hands aye heavy in just visitations,
    By all earth's nations
    Most reverenced, come !

ATHENA.

Glad am I for my land
Thus dowered with gracious hand.
  I bless the soft eyes' pleading   970
  Of Suasion : when, not heeding
  Mine own lips' interceding,
These raged, she spake through me.
'Twas Zeus the Counsel-lord
Gained us that great award.
  Henceforth in rivalry
Of good deeds we contending
Shall both, through years unending
    Win victory.

CHORUS. *(Ant. 2)*

And faction, hungry for mischief ever,
    In your streets never
    Resound her yell;
Nor may burghers' blood from the red dust crying, 980
    With murders replying
    To murders, swell
The tale of curses; but love delighting
    In love-requiting
    Be theirs: one will
In cherishing friends, against foemen steeling
    Their hearts—here is healing
    For many an ill.

ATHENA.

Lo, wisdom in the hearts of these;
    Their tongues the law of kindness learn.
Great gain from these dread Presences   990
    For this my people I discern.
These love you now; O love them ye;
    Honour ye them exceedingly:
So all your lives shall be with glory crowned—
A land, a state, for righteousness renowned.

CHORUS. *(Str. 3)*

Blessèd be ye in your goodly heritage, burgher-nation!
    Blessèd be ye, who are homed so nigh unto Zeus,
        who are dear
To the Maiden beloved, with her wisdom are dowered,
      to whose habitation   1000
    'Neath the wings of Pallas, the bolts of Allfather
    come not near.

ATHENA.

Blessèd be ye withal!
Now must I pass before, to lead you
    On to your shrine-crypt's hall.
Lo where the sacred lamps precede you
High-borne by your attendant-train.
By blood of hallowed victims slain
On-ushered pass ye underground.
    Thence send ye influences benign,
    That victory's star on these may shine:
    Each influence to my land malign
    Be there fast bound.
Lead, warders of my city-home,   1010
Ye sons of Kranaus, these who come
To sojourn with you.   In my folk
Aye may their gracious acts provoke
    Love: be your hearts their shrine!

CHORUS.   *(Ant. 3)*

Blessèd be ye, twice-blessèd, all ye in the city abiding,
  O ye Immortals and mortals, who dwell within
      Pallas's wall!
While ye shall revere me, your fellow-abider, no cause
    for chiding
  Of the lot of your life shall ye find, what chance
    soever befall.   1020

ATHENA.

All praise to these your invocation-vows!
With light of splendour-bearing brands will I
Escort you to your deep haunts 'neath the earth,
I and mine handmaids, who with reverence ward
My sacred image.   Of all Theseus' land

Now shall the flower go forth, a glorious troop
Of boys, of women, and of matrons old.
With crimson vesture's bravery honour ye
These.   Let the leaping flames set forward now,
That these, our land's great visitants, may show 1030
Their grace henceforth in fair prosperity.

*The procession of women and children, headed by
Athena and the Eumenides, moves forward.*

CHANT OF THE ESCORT-PROCESSION. *(Str. 1)*

Pass to your homes, O Mighty Ones, of honour jealous
    ever,
Sprung from Night's womb, lone Powers, of whom
    shall spring like issue never;
        Led on by this adoring train—
*O dwellers in the land, refrain from speech : this hush
    is holy !—*

(Ant. 1)
Pass to the immemorial caves, hid under earth dark-
    veiling :
There upon you with honours due, with sacrifice
    unfailing,
        Shall we in deepest reverence call.
*Break silence not, ye people all; from speech refrain
    you wholly !*

*The procession reaches the entrance to the Cave of
the Furies, which is beneath the Areopagus.*

(Str. 2)
Come hither, Queens of Worship, come, henceforth
    on Athens turning   1040